"This is a very good book, full of historiographical wisdom. I recommend it strongly as a sure and encouraging guide to budding historians befuddled by the so-called 'history wars,' and to anyone who is interested in the challenges attending those who represent the history of Christian thought."

Douglas A. Sweeney, Chair and Professor of Church History & History of Christian Thought Department, Trinity Evangelical Divinity School; Director, Jonathan Edwards Center

"Carl Trueman's cogent and engaging approach to historiography provides significant examples of problems faced by historians and the kinds of fallacies frequently encountered in historical argumentation. Trueman steers a clear path between problematic and overdrawn conclusions on the one hand and claims of utter objectivity on the other. His illustrations, covering several centuries of Western history, are telling. He offers a combination of careful historical analysis coupled with an understanding of the logical and argumentative pitfalls to which historians are liable that is a service to the field and should provide a useful guide to beginning researchers. A must for courses on research methodology."

Richard Muller, P. J. Zondervan Professor of Historical Theology Emeritus, Calvin Theological Seminary

"Because the past shapes the present, a just understanding of the past is important for any individual, society, or church. Here is wise and practical advice for those wanting to write history for others about how to do it well. Follow this guidance and avoid the pitfalls!"

David Bebbington, Professor of History, University of Stirling

Histories and Fallacies

Histories and Fallacies

PROBLEMS FACED IN
THE WRITING OF HISTORY

CARL R. TRUEMAN

:: CROSSWAY®

WHEATON, ILLINOIS

Histories and Fallacies: Problems Faced in the Writing of History
Copyright © 2010 by Carl R. Trueman
Published by Crossway
   1300 Crescent Street
   Wheaton, Illinois 60187

Interior design and typesetting: Lakeside Design Plus
Cover image: Photographic visiting card of Karl Marx (1818–93) with his signature (photo) by French School (19th century) Musee de L'Histoire Vivante, Montreuil, France/ Archives Charmet/ The Bridgeman Art Library
First printing 2010
Printed in the United States of America

Scripture quotations are from the ESV® Bible (*The Holy Bible, English Standard Version*®), copyright © 2001 by Crossway. Used by permission. All rights reserved.

Trade Paperback ISBN: 978-1-58134-923-8
PDF ISBN: 978-1-4335-1263-6
Mobipocket ISBN: 978-1-4335-1264-3
ePub ISBN: 978-1-4335-2080-8

Library of Congress Cataloging-in-Publication Data
 Trueman, Carl R.
  Histories and fallacies : problems faced in the writing of history / Carl R. Trueman.
   p. cm.
  Includes bibliographical references.
  ISBN 978-1-58134-923-8 (trade pbk.)—ISBN 978-1-4335-1263-6 (PDF)
 —ISBN 978-1-4335-1264-3 (Mobipocket)—ISBN 978-1-4335-2080-8 (ePub)
 1. Historiography—Handbooks, manuals, etc. 2. History—Philosophy. 3. History—Methodology. 4. History—Errors, inventions, etc. I. Title.
 D13.T74 2010
 907.2—dc22   2010021878

Crossway is a publishing ministry of Good News Publishers.

CH 27 26 25 24 23 22 21 20 19 18 17

In Memory of John Harry Trueman
1939–2008
Who first taught me to love stories.
The rest, as they say, is history.

Contents

Acknowledgments	11
Introduction	13
1. The Denial of History	25
2. Grand Schemes and Misdemeanors	69
3. The Past Is a Foreign Country	109
4. A Fistful of Fallacies	141
Concluding Historical Postscript	169
Appendix: The Reception of Calvin: Historical Considerations	183

Acknowledgments

This book is one that I had wanted to write for some time. I have always loved all kinds of history, and so when Allan Fisher offered me the opportunity to write on topics outside of my immediate area of specialization, such as Holocaust Denial and Marxism, the temptation was irresistible. Thanks therefore go to Allan for commissioning the volume; to Justin Taylor for suggesting the idea in the first place; and to all the staff at Crossway who have been both very patient with the constant delays to the book and so efficient in expediting the process once I had finished the manuscript. As always, I am indebted to my colleagues in Academic Affairs at Westminster, Mrs. Becky Lippert and Mrs. Leah Stapleton, who have shouldered much of the administrative burden so that I have been free to pursue my writing projects. Finally, my wife and children have, as always, proved a constant source of encouragement and inspiration.

One reason for the book's delay was the death of my father in July 2008. The book is dedicated to his memory.

Introduction

Why write a book on how to do history? This is without a doubt a good question, especially for me. For many years, I looked with withering contempt on those who wrote such books, my philosophy being something like a historian's version of George Bernard Shaw's attitude to teachers: those who *can* write history, *do* write history; those who cannot, write books telling others how to do it. Yet, after spending much of the last twenty years involved in some form or another in the writing and teaching of history, I have come to the conclusion that there is a place for books that reflect on the nature of the historical task.

To explain this, I need to offer a little autobiographical reflection. For as long as I can remember, I have enjoyed stories. As a child, I was entranced by the epics of ancient mythology—the adventures of Odysseus, the Trojan War, and the antics of pagan gods, be they Egyptian, Greek, or Norse. I also loved the stories contained in the Arabian Nights, the Icelandic sagas, and the various other collections of myths and legends that I found on my father's bookcase or in the local library. Indeed, some of my earliest memories are of my father reading Dickens's neglected work, *A Child's History of England*, to me as I went to bed at night. I have never lost this love, and still enjoy nothing better than reading this kind of epic material; but as I grew up, I also broadened my tastes to include a much wider taste in literature, from Thomas Hardy to Raymond Chandler. If there was a good story out there, I wanted to read it.

Strange to tell, I came rather late to history, in the last two years of my studies on the Classical Tripos at the University of Cambridge. I had chosen Classics for a number of reasons: I was good at Latin, and had the typical state grammar schoolboy's attitude of focusing on what I did well and abandoning that which I found boring; and, of course, in studying Classics, I could spend my time reading all those things I enjoyed—the Homeric epics, the tales of gods and heroes, the great myths and legends of the classical world. History was not a motivating factor: at school it had always seemed to be an endless list of names and dates and statistics, with the result that, again as a typical grammar schoolboy, I applied myself minimally to it and did not take it further than the fifth form (that's age sixteen, for American readers). But at Cambridge, all that changed. The 1980s were a great time to be doing Classics at this university. Under the brilliant lectures of Keith Hopkins and Paul Millet and the breathtaking supervision of Paul Cartledge, I suddenly realized that at the heart of history was the telling of stories that explained the past. There were a variety of such stories—economic, social, cultural, military, etc.—but far from being a dry collection of names, dates, and places, history could possess all the narrative excitement of the epic myths I loved so well; more than that, these stories were attempts to wrestle with the past in a way that tried to explain why things had happened the way they had. Paul Cartledge was particularly impressive. Basically a Marxist historian (who has since gone on not only to hold a chair at Cambridge but also to become something of a "television don," with a number of acclaimed series, including one on Sparta, to his credit), Dr. Cartledge told the story of ancient Greece from the perspective of class struggle, a perspective to which Athens was not particularly susceptible but which bore great fruit in studies of Sparta, his own chosen area of specialization, whose social organization lent itself to precisely such analysis. Even those who disagree with his approach would have to concede that what he offered was a cogent, coherent account of the ancient Greek world, put forth in the public domain, open for all to see, to agree with, or to criticize.

Since my time at Cambridge, my love for history has known no bounds. I often tell people that I have the greatest job in the world: I am paid to tell stories. The stories I tell happen to relate to the history of the church, but, frankly, I could have studied any aspect of the past and enjoyed doing it. And, in my classes, I spend little time hammering names and dates in the abstract into my students; they can get that from the textbooks I recommend. That's the purpose of textbooks: to cover the boring material so that the lecturer does not have to, but rather is free to focus on the discipline's more interesting aspects. I do not teach timelines; I try instead to engage students by showing them how to construct narratives of the past in a way that unlocks that past for an audience in the present.

But this is where key questions for the historian start to come into play. I have said above that I loved the stories in the Greek myths and the Arabian Nights. I have also said that I loved the stories of histories, be they of the kings of ancient Sparta, the emperors of Rome, the French Revolution, or the cataclysms of the twentieth century. But what is the difference? Indeed, is there any difference between, let's say, Homer's account of Odysseus's travels and Richard Evans's account of the rise of the Third Reich?

Most would probably respond: of course there is. The Third Reich actually happened; the adventures of Odysseus are a myth, at best of tenuous relationship to anything that really occurred in the ancient world. So far, so good; but the last half century has witnessed a veritable earthquake in the field of the historical discipline, which has brought such a simple, straightforward, common-sense answer into serious question. To put the problem succinctly and simply, the question has been raised in various forms as to how we know the stories being told us by historians are reliable. Given the historian's constructive role in the storytelling and the fact that no story is either identical with the past (a story is, after all, not the events themselves, but words, whether spoken or written) or an exhaustive account of the past (everyone has a perspective, and everyone is selective in what they include and exclude), does not every historical narrative become unavoidably relative compared to any other?

This crisis in confidence in the historical profession can be illustrated with reference to two recent phenomena. The first is a bill introduced to the Florida state legislature in 2006 by the state's then governor, Jeb Bush, which was intended to have an immediate impact upon the way history is taught. Here is how the matter was reported on one news Web page, starting with a quotation from the text of the bill itself:

> "American history shall be viewed as factual, not constructed, shall be viewed as knowable, teachable, and testable, and shall be defined as the creation of a new nation based largely on the universal principles stated in the Declaration of Independence." To that end teachers are charged not only to focus on the history and content of the Declaration but are also instructed to teach the "history, meaning, significance and effect of the provisions of the Constitution of the United States and the amendments thereto...." Other bill provisions place new emphasis on "flag education, including proper flag display and flag salute" and on the need to teach "the nature and importance of free enterprise to the United States economy.[1]

The bill as it stands would appear to be an attempt to hit back at that kind of radical relativism which, in its crudest form (and not a form one finds very often) declares that all narratives are equally true and valid, and that the writing of history is really just the projection of individual viewpoints. It is also, of course, arguable that it is an example of precisely the kind of approach to history that the relativists seek to critique: that which intentionally privileges its own position with the status of "just the facts," and effectively reduces the number of valid accounts of history to its own version, while tarring others with the brush of being political inventions of those out to subvert the status quo. If the narrative is to focus, for example, on "the nature and importance of free enterprise to the United States economy," it would seem to be a small step indeed between the telling of history and the advocating of a particular economic philosophy,

---

[1] History News Network, "New Florida Law Tightens Control over History in Schools," http://hnn. us/roundup/entries/26016.html (accessed August 21, 2006).

which just happened to be that of the governor of Florida. Further, even if we discount what would seem to be an obvious political agenda behind this pedagogical legislation, can we reduce history just to the parameters set therein? What about the history of art or of literature? What about approaches that focus on economics, or ethnicity, or immigration patterns? Are none of these worth studying? Are there no valid histories that can be built around these things?

In short, the proposed Florida legislation seems to make two basic mistakes: it fails to understand that history is not simply a collation of facts which can only be related together in one valid narrative; and it restricts the number of worthwhile topics of study, and, indeed does so in a way that seems to smuggle the conclusion in to the very premise. Politicians generally make bad academics, of course, so we should not be too hard on the idiotic nature of such statements. Yet, for all of its obvious flaws, the proposed legislation does have at its heart something that is a very valid concern: to rule out of bounds the possibility that there are a potentially infinite number of sometimes contradictory yet equally valid ways of talking about the past. The attempt may be ham-fisted, overblown, and inept, but at heart it is trying to make the point that some accounts of history are more true and more valid than others.

This is where the second example is instructive, that of Holocaust Denial (HD). I want to look at HD in somewhat more detail in chapter 1; for now, it is sufficient to note it as a phenomenon. There is an old adage among historians that no event in history is so certain that, sooner or later, somebody won't come along and deny that it ever happened. One can think of numerous examples. Take, for example, the death of Elvis. Did he really die in 1977? Well, television reports seem to indicate that he did, as does the death certificate; and I myself have stood by the graveside in Graceland and seen the headstone, the existence of which is typically, though not absolutely, a sign that, yes, the person whose name is on the stone is dead and buried beneath. Yet theories abound: that he is alive and well and working as a shelf-stacker in a supermarket; or that he's hiding in the second story of the Graceland mansion (which is suspiciously cordoned off to keep visitors out). My point here is not about silly conspiracy theories, but about the fact that even what would appear to be obvious historical truths are often challenged—and then the question becomes how one adjudicates between competing versions of events. In fact, can one ever so adjudicate? Is my narrative of Elvis's death simply my truth, and my neighbor's narrative of Elvis's continued gainful employment at the local Wawa his truth?

This example is, of course, absurd and trivial—unless, that is, one happens actually to be Elvis or one of his relatives—but there has been a trend over recent decades toward a kind of epistemological nihilism that has so relativized everything that access to the past in any meaningful way is virtually denied; and the more this is the case, the harder it is to argue that the statement "Elvis died in 1977" is a more accurate historical claim than "Elvis spent 2008 working in the Cricklewood Community Center."

The implications of this can, of course, be much more serious than statements about the current community contributions of "the King." HD is much more disturbing, both because of its moral implications and because the Holocaust was such a vast event which, one would assume, left a huge amount of historical evidence behind from which to piece together what actually happened. Much of history can be said to be of relatively little immediate consequence; but the Holocaust involved the systematic destruction of human life on a vast scale and continues to shape current events, such as attitudes to the nation-state of Israel. Thus, denying the Holocaust has a clear moral dimension that, say, denying the death of Elvis does not. Further, given the vast amount of apparent evidence for the Holocaust—documentary, photographic, eyewitness, physical—to deny it requires not simply a dramatic revision of established historical wisdom but a wholesale inversion of the same; and, to any casual observer, its denial represents a direct challenge to normal canons of evidence. If historians have tricked us into believing the Holocaust has happened, can we be certain of anything they say?

HD hit the headlines in a most dramatic way in 2000, when British historian David Irving sued American professor Deborah Lipstadt for claiming in her book, *Denying the Holocaust*, that he was a Holocaust denier.[2] Irving chose the British venue because, unlike the American legal code, English libel law does not require proof of malicious intent, and thus he was more likely to obtain a judgment in his favor. What this case did was put on the public stage, in a dramatic fashion, questions that had been perplexing the historical profession for decades: can history tell the truth? Are some narratives more true than others? Can one demonstrate that some claims are simply false? Of course, historical method cannot be established as correct by some legal verdict; but the case provided a unique and, by its context, very exciting opportunity for historians at the top of their game to demonstrate how careful sifting of the various types of evidence available could be used to establish the basic truth that the Holocaust did indeed happen. It also served as a salutary reminder that the game historians play in lecture rooms and seminars, often over matters that are in themselves of no earthly significance, can have important and sometimes frightening implications in the real world. True, Holocaust deniers are far from being postmodernists in their own approach to evidence—they believe that the evidence supports their thesis—but their existence challenges the mainstream historical profession: do our methods and approaches offer us any means of dismantling their arguments?

Still, we are getting ahead of ourselves. The ins and outs of HD will be discussed in greater detail below where we will see that a discussion of HD is extraordinarily instructive in understanding some of the worst fallacies committed by historians. Suffice it to say here, however, that these two examples, the rather wooden but well-intentioned legislation in the state of Florida and the distasteful phenomenon of HD, are prime examples of why good historical method is crucial: we need to avoid the naïveté that just sees history as something "out there," which we simply dig up and drop into the specimen jar, and the radical epistemological nihilism of those who think that all historical narratives are simply subjective or social constructions that cannot be assessed in relation to each other. As a trio of distinguished UCLA historians expressed the matter:

---

[2]Deborah Lipstadt, *Denying the Holocaust: The Growing Assault on Truth and Memory* (New York: Penguin, 1994).

The relativist argument about history is analogous to the claim that because definitions of child abuse or schizophrenia have altered over time, in that sense having been socially constructed, then neither can be said to exist in any meaningful way.[3]

The point is well made. It is one thing for historians to play about with notions of epistemological nihilism in the classroom; it is quite another to tell the victim of abuse that such a thing is merely a linguistic construct, a point that may well not be intended as a denial of the victim's suffering, yet the philosophical subtlety of which is surely lost in translation, so to speak. Yet in order to avoid this radical constructionism, historians need to spend some time reflecting upon the nature of their discipline and upon the limits of what can be done with historical evidence and interpretation.

There are historians who have made a veritable career out of writing books on how to do history while rarely seeming to have gotten around to doing any for themselves. I trust I will not become such; obsession with method is one of the baleful aspects of modern literary theory, and it has not served society well in promoting the reading or writing of literature. Nevertheless, some level of methodological self-awareness is important for those engaged in the writing of history. It can help one understand the nature of evidence, of how much weight can be placed on any single artifact, on what questions can legitimately be asked of certain texts, of how one should select evidence, and what the implications of such selectivity are for the history one then writes.

In order to explore these questions, I have chosen in this book to look at a series of problems relative to the writing of history that can be explored with reference to specific questions and examples. My hope is that, by doing so, readers will not so much buy into some nebulous "Trueman method" for doing history but will be caused to reflect upon how they themselves approach the subject and, even if they find no reason to change that approach, will at least become more self-aware and intentional about it.

---

[3]Joyce Appleby, Lynn Hunt, and Margaret Jacob, *Telling the Truth about History* (New York: Norton, 1994), 6.

In chapter 1, I examine the issue of objectivity in history, using Holocaust Denial as my specific example. Given the fact that no historian is a blank page and that the writing of history is an action of an individual living at a certain time and a certain place, working with all of the personal and cultural baggage that this brings in its wake, we will ask whether the fact that no history can be neutral ultimately means that all historical narratives are inevitably so biased and relative that their claims to historical truth are meaningless. My conclusion is that, while there is no such thing as neutrality in the telling of history, there is such a thing as objectivity, and that varied interpretations of historical evidence are yet susceptible to generally agreed upon procedures of verification that allow us to challenge each others' readings of the evidence. You might believe that action X is a clear example of class struggle; but I can challenge you by looking at the evidence to see whether your interpretation is plausible, given the status of the evidence. I also argue that all histories are provisional in the sense that no one can offer an exhaustive account of any past action, given the limited state of the evidence and the historian's inevitably limited grasp of context as well as distance from the past. But provisional merely means limited and subject to refinement; it does not make all readings of the evidence equally valid, or equally unreliable.

In chapter 2, building on the discussion in chapter 1, we will examine issues relating to the idea of interpretative frameworks, those general models of historical action and meaning which historians bring to bear on their task and which shape both the selection and interpretation of evidence. There are various models that I could use as an example of this, but I am going to focus on the one with which I am most familiar: Marxism, particularly as it finds its expression in the works of seventeenth-century British historian Christopher Hill. The purpose of this chapter is not to disparage the notion of grand theory or the kind of schemes of which Marxism is just one of the better-known examples; rather it is to highlight both the strengths and weaknesses of such an approach. On the positive side, Marxism raises awareness of issues that may be hidden below the surface of historical events, and it provides a helpful framework for identifying, collating, and interpreting evidence. On the negative side, it has built into it elements that render it immune to criticism and thus cause it to fall foul of the principle of falsification. Nevertheless, as I will show with a couple of examples, the importance of material factors in shaping historical action is something which Marxism highlights and which is useful even to those who are not committed to Marxist ideology.

In chapter 3, we will address the problem of anachronism. Anachronism is a constant temptation for historians and, to an extent, unavoidable. The writing of history involves a historian in the present addressing questions to the past; inevitably, that involves the bringing together, if not collision, of two different periods in time, with all of the difficulties that brings in its wake. The problem is particularly acute in my own specialist field, that of the history of ideas, where the desire to plunder the past for precedents for present thinking is often a subtle, even imperceptible, pressure that can dramatically impoverish, if not utterly distort, the historical task. In my own thinking in this area, I have been immensely helped by the methodological reflections of Quentin Skinner, and thus examination of his arguments and contributions will be central to the discussion. We will also look at the problem of using anachronistic categories.

In chapter 4, I address what I have called "a fistful of fallacies." This is far from an exhaustive treatment of all the fallacies to which historians can be prone; nor, to be honest, is every issue addressed therein a "fallacy" in the strict sense of the word. Rather, it is a collection of reflections on particular issues of which the historian should be aware. Most historians, in my experience, just think of themselves as doing history; and there is much to be said for the avoidance of the frankly pretentious and obscurantist language that is so often used by those who spend their time not so much writing history themselves as reflecting on the "theory" of history. Too often representatives of the latter caste are committed to demonstrating that what clearly works in practice cannot work in theory, a rather bizarre, parasitic, and frankly contemptible way to spend one's life. Having said that, all of us as historians can benefit from being more self-aware about the things we do. There are logical and linguistic mistakes that, once we are aware of them, we are less likely to commit; and this chapter is intended as a guide to them.

Finally, the book concludes with an appendix, a paper delivered at a conference on the reception of John Calvin's thought, reflecting upon the problems surrounding the connection of thoughts and actions in one era with those in another. Much has been made of the notions of continuity and discontinuity in Christian thought over recent years, and this chapter represents an attempt to address the questions that this raises. It thus stands as an example of methodological reflection on a specific issue in contemporary historical studies.

My approach in this book is, on the whole, to emphasize historians in action and spend less time talking about theory. Theory has enjoyed something of a boom over the last twenty years, to the point where there are now historians who appear to spend all their time writing books about the theory of writing history and rarely do any actual writing of history. While I once used to drive a hard wedge between historians and those who philosophize about history, I have softened over the years and am now fully committed to the idea that every historian needs to be methodologically self-aware and self-critical; yet I still believe that *doing* history is the historian's primary calling and the thing that he or she should do best. Thus, the reader will find little discussion of the latest critical theories of history and much of the practicalities of writing history, illustrated with examples. The result is not a scholarly work aimed to impress the critical theorists out there; rather I trust it will be a guide to the perplexed, a useful handbook that will serve to make good students of history more aware of why they are good students of history, and others aware of things they can do to raise their game.

It is my hope that, by the end of the book, readers will have more awareness of the role they themselves play in the writing of history and of the strengths and the limits of the historical task in which they are engaged. As I have already said at the start, there is part of me that thinks that those who *can* do history, *do* history; yet, even if nothing I say makes you change how you do history, I trust you will be more self-aware in the way you practice the discipline and this in itself will prove of benefit. Once one knows why and how one thinks and acts the way one does, one is able to sharpen and improve in greater measure than before.

Ultimately, for me, all good historians, no matter what the period which they study, are engaged in asking variations on a basic question: why is this person doing this thing in this way in this place at this particular point in time? Once you realize that that is the kind of question you have been asking all along, you are free to answer it more effectively and to hone your methods to that question more accurately and precisely. The result is better historical consciousness, method, and, hopefully, writing. I trust that this book will provide the reader with some of the key tools to enable such an outcome.

CHAPTER 1

The Denial of History

One of the popular clichés of contemporary culture is that all truth is relative. As one pop song once expressed it, "This is my truth, now tell me yours." This relativism has manifested itself within the historical profession over recent decades in terms of a rising epistemological skepticism, if not nihilism, that has tended in the most extreme cases to make all narratives simply projections of the present-day circumstances and opinions of the historian. This has been fuelled in part by the impact of some trends in continental philosophy and literary theory, and also by an increasing realization that the historian's situatedness, choice of subject, selection of evidence, etc., all have an impact on the nature of the historical narrative that is being constructed. It is now generally accepted that no history is "neutral," in the sense that it just gives you the facts. Said facts are selected and then fitted together into a narrative by historians who have their own particular viewpoints and their own particular ways of doing things. For example, if I were to sit down and write the history of the French Revolution, various factors would shape the final product: my nationality;

my particular approach (am I interested in economics, or literature, or politics?); perhaps even my own views on whether monarchies are a good idea—all of these things will impact how I write and what conclusions I draw. After all, history is not simply "the past" but is a *representation* of the past by someone in the present; and a history of the French Revolution is a representation of the events to which that term refers by someone who has a variety of commitments that impact the historical task. As John Lukacs defines history, it is "the remembered past," and as such is inevitably shaped by those who do the remembering.

In this context, claims to neutrality are vulnerable to the kind of criticism launched by Nietzsche in the nineteenth century, and which also resonates with the thought of those other great masters of modern suspicion, Sigmund Freud and Karl Marx: the claim to neutrality is merely a specious means of privileging my point of view—disguised as the simple truth, so to speak—over that of everybody else. I have truth, pure and simple; they have spin, propaganda, hidden agendas, etc. And, even if we do not go all the way with the criticism of a Nietzsche or a Marx, we must acknowledge at the outset that history written without a standpoint is not simply practically impossible—it is also logically inconceivable.

But does this acknowledgment that no history is *neutral* therefore require that all histories are, ultimately, biased to such an extent that we must acknowledge the validity of all? Is the history that says that John Lennon died in 1980 as valid as the history that claims that he was kidnapped by the CIA and is being held prisoner in Guantanamo Bay? Our instinctive reaction is to say no, of course not. But then the question must be asked: can we justify that claim? Why do we hold that the former is true and the latter false? If no history is neutral, then why can I not resolve the differences in these two narratives by seeing them in terms of the viewpoints of the two historians?

It is in this context that an important distinction needs to be made: the distinction between neutrality and objectivity. Only when this distinction is understood can we begin to see how we can acknowledge the valid insights of much modern and postmodern critical thinking about the practice of history while yet avoid the kind of epistemological anarchy that some would wish to see wreak havoc.

Objectivity Is Not Neutrality

In a popular book on the Old Testament and Ancient Near Eastern literature, Peter Enns asks the following question: "Is there really any such thing as a completely objective and unbiased recording of history, modern or premodern?"[1] The question is posed rhetorically—after all, what fool would today answer in the affirmative?—and it seems, at first glance, to be a good one; but it also contains a huge assumption that is highly problematic. Perhaps it is unfair to expect a scholar of biblical languages to be familiar with debates from within the historical field, but the assumption that Enns makes is that *objective* and *unbiased* seem to be two words for the same thing; and, of course, on the grounds that nobody today would argue for the unbiased nature of any historical writing, the implication is that nobody can argue for the objective nature of historical writing either. Yet most historians would, I believe, both acknowledge the biased nature of the history they write and also maintain that they aspire to be objective in what they do. As we shall see below, the fact that Richard Evans and David Irving approach the Holocaust from specific viewpoints and perspectives does not mean that their respective histories are equally valid; there are ways and means of comparing them that indicate that nonneutrality does not equate to solipsistic subjectivity.

In an impressive study of the American historical profession, Robert Novick has shown that the search for objectivity has been the chimerical goal of the profession for over a century.[2] His argument is interesting, not least because he does demonstrate how the ideal of objectivity itself has been transformed over the years. In the late nineteenth century, it is arguable that the notions of objectivity and neutrality were essentially the same thing, with

---

[1] Peter Enns, *Inspiration and Incarnation: Evangelicals and the Problem of the Old Testament* (Grand Rapids: Baker, 2005), 45.
[2] Peter Novick, *That Noble Dream: The "Objectivity Question" and the American Historical Profession* (Cambridge: Cambridge University Press, 1988).

the terms being virtually interchangeable. Over the years, however, a gap has opened up between them. In addition, as at least one significant reviewer pointed out, there is an interesting disjunction in the book between what Novick *says* and what he actually *does*. On the face of it, his argument is that the quest for objectivity is a fool's errand; yet this argument is made in a book which, for me as for numerous other historians, meets what we would regard as decent standards of objectivity. The book is surely not neutral, but its argument is testable by public criteria and demonstrates precisely the kind of method and approach to the evidence that could be described as objective. Sure, Novick has his biases; he is no more able to divest himself of his own prior commitments and opinions and analytical frameworks than anybody else. But he does not write gnostic history that only he and his followers can understand; his arguments are public ones that can be evaluated by others. In arguing against the possibility of objectivity, then, Novick has produced a first-class piece of objective scholarship, a point made pungently by one of his appreciative critics![3]

At the heart of the historian's task is this matter of verifiability and accountability by public criteria, and the criticism of Novick's approach is to the point: there is a lot of postmodern rhetoric around about the possibility of history and of representing the past, but the bottom line is that most historians do acknowledge in their procedures and methods that such public criteria do exist, and that it is practically possible to make a distinction between a history that asserts that Henry V defeated the French at Agincourt and a history that would even deny the very existence of Henry V. Thus, to demonstrate what is at stake, let us now turn to an extreme modern example of history that is really no history at all.

The Ultimate Test Case: The Holocaust

It is, of course, one thing to play academic games with notions of history, neutrality, and objectivity, but quite another to see where this can lead in

---

[3] Thomas L. Haskell, "Objectivity Is Not Neutrality: Rhetoric versus Practice in Peter Novick's *That Noble Dream*" in *Objectivity Is Not Neutrality: Explanatory Schemes in History* (Baltimore: Johns Hopkins University Press, 1998), 145–73.

its most extreme form. The most notorious example of this is the phenomenon of Holocaust Denial (HD), an approach to the history of the Nazi genocide in Europe between 1933 and 1945 that dramatically downplays the number of people killed and rejects the notion that there was any organized and state-sanctioned campaign of mass murder. To many it seems incredible that such arguments could ever be made with any plausibility; but if historical knowledge is impossible in any ultimate sense, then the Holocaust too, vast and well-documented as it would appear to be, is also negotiable as an object of our knowledge and narratives.

Before we look at how HD functions in terms of historical method, a few preliminary comments are in order. First, it is important to understand that those who argue for HD are generally not radical postmodernists who are skeptical of all claims to historical knowledge. They may deny the Holocaust, but they do not deny the possibility of historical knowledge. Far from it. In fact, the very opposite is the case: they want to argue that the accepted narratives of the Holocaust are wrong, demonstrably wrong, and that their alternative narratives are demonstrably true—or at least more true and coherent as interpretations of the evidence.

Second, the issue with HD is therefore not that its advocates propose a postmodern method; HD is rather a challenge to the mainstream historical guild and its flirtatious relationship with postmodern skepticism. This is where the postmodern question of the nature of knowledge comes in. We must all acknowledge that, as no history is neutral, so no history of the Holocaust can be neutral. But does that mean we have to concede that all accounts of it are equally valid or deserve a place at the table? Is HD a problem of historical method, or merely of taste? Can historians reject HD on the grounds that it represents flawed historical method that is demonstrably problematic by objective criteria? Or must we do it simply on the grounds that its results and implications are morally repugnant and distasteful by the ethical and aesthetic standards of the day? This is a pressing question. Whether King Alfred really burned the cakes is an interesting historical question, but its moral implications are minimal and of concern only to the lady whose cakes he was supposed to be watching; whether Jews really were gassed and cremated in Auschwitz has far more dramatic and perennial moral implications for everything from current international policies in the Middle East to how we understand the evil potential of human nature and technology.

Third, while we can all have suspicions as to why advocates of HD, from Paul Rassinier to Rousas J. Rushdoony to David Irving, think the way they do about the Holocaust, we need to remember that it is not a historian's motivation which renders his or her analysis invalid; it is improper use and interpretation of evidence which does so.[4] Thus, the fact that Irving, for example, has spoken for extreme neo-Nazi-style groups does not necessarily mean that he is a bad historian, any more than, say, Eric Hobsbawm's or Christopher Hill's membership in the Communist Party necessarily renders all their historical contributions negligible or invalid.

We should also, at this point, comment briefly on mainstream Holocaust scholarship in order to understand in more detail the precise claims of HD. Although the Holocaust is, inevitably, a very sensitive area, the scholarship is not monolithic and does represent a diversity of viewpoints. For example, estimates of the number of those killed vary from around five million to above ten million. By its very nature, the evidence defies a precise and universally agreed figure, unlike, say, the evidence for the number of tickets sold to a sporting event. It is, however, clear that figures of, say, eight hundred thousand, are woefully inadequate as accounts of the numbers involved. Such a figure would, on established legal definitions, constitute HD.[5]

More significantly, mainstream Holocaust historians can be divided into two basic camps: intentionalists and functionalists. Intentionalists argue that the program of genocide, with all of the organizational structures it

---

[4]While Rushdoony's followers do not like to acknowledge his Holocaust Denial, it is incontestable that he held such a position, according to the technical definition (i.e., a massive lowering of the number of estimated dead from the usual six million and rejection of the idea of systematic mass slaughter). His sources are atrocious, secondhand, and unverified; that he held this position speaks volumes about his appalling incompetence as a historian, and one can only speculate as to why he held the position from a moral perspective: see his *The Institutes of Biblical Law* (Phillipsburg: Presbyterian and Reformed, 1973), 586–88. He deals with the matter under the issue of the ninth commandment and, ironically breaches it himself in his presentation of the matter.

[5]For a classic account of the Holocaust, see Martin Gilbert, *The Holocaust: A History of the Jews of Europe during the Second World War* (New York: Henry Holt, 1985).

involved, was the result of a clear plan from early in the Nazi regime. In other words, the death camps and the systematic and total annihilation of the European Jews had been the intention all along. All that happened in the thirties and early forties was part of a larger, coherent policy that aimed to rid Europe of the Jews by mass deportation and destruction.

The functionalists, however, see the program of genocide as evolving over time, and the result, if not exactly an accident, was not part of the original Nazi intention. In other words, the death camps developed out of the ongoing anti-Semitic program and were not the original end goal. The concept of Auschwitz and the other death camps was not something in the mind of the leading Nazis when they were swept to power in 1933; rather, the development of the mechanisms of totalitarianism, the increasingly organized and violent anti-Semitic policies of the state, the hostile expansion to the east, the development of technology, and the failure of other schemes (such as Adolf Eichmann's hare-brained scheme to send all the Jews to Madagascar), little by little led the Nazis down a path that culminated in the Final Solution as agreed upon at the infamous Wannsee Conference on January 20, 1942, when the policy of highly organized and technologically executed genocide was approved.

The existence of intentionalists and functionalists is significant because it highlights a couple of things. First, it indicates that there are matters upon which the evidence is open to a variety of legitimate but different interpretations. Some documents point to longstanding intention; others seem to imply a more *ad hoc* program. It is perhaps not exactly "you pay your money and take your choice," but there is room here for historians to disagree about exactly what the documents seem to be saying.

This leads us to the second point: there are areas of evidence where, quite frankly, there is no legitimate room for disagreement, and it is this notion of legitimate versus illegitimate interpretations that will most upset the consistent radical relativists of the postmodern historical guild. They may, to one degree or another, accept that there are *morally* legitimate and illegitimate interpretations (though it is arguable that even this category might itself be merely a bid for power), but to delimit the range of meanings of a text or an artifact by notions of historical meaning is counter to the excesses of the postmodern historical mindset. The questions addressed by this are crucial: were most Holocaust deaths the result of the winter cold in the east? Were there gas chambers at Auschwitz? Did Eichmann mastermind the logistics of transporting Jews from across Europe to camps created specifically to murder them? Did the Wannsee Conference take place and set the final stage for the systematic genocide on a massive scale? If these points cannot be established on the base of the massive documentary and artifactual evidence we have, then realistically speaking there can be no historical knowledge of anything and we are now living in the ultimate Cartesian nightmare where the only thing I can (probably!) be certain of is my own existence. Thankfully, on the answers to these matters, there is no meaningful, competent, and coherent dissent, any more than there is on whether the moon is made of green cheese.

Thus, to summarize: setting aside postmodern relativist rhetoric, and also questions about how the Holocaust is and is not used in contemporary political discourse, there is a hard core of public material that historians agree is pertinent evidence for understanding the Holocaust, and while this evidence is open to a variety of interpretations, it is not open to an infinite range of interpretations. This needs to be held in mind as we move to discuss the details of HD.

A Brief Introduction to the World of Holocaust Denial

There are a number of very good accounts of the history and culture of Holocaust Denial. The most famous is Deborah Lipstadt's *Denying the Holocaust: The Growing Assault on Truth and Memory*. Lipstadt, herself Jewish, was catapulted to fame when David Irving, named in the book as an advocate of HD, sued her in a British court in 2000. The trial transcripts are conveniently available online, with a host of other relevant material, at Emory University's "Holocaust Denial on Trial" site, but two other books emerged from the legal proceedings that make exciting reads.[6] The first is *History on Trial: My Day in Court with a Holocaust Denier*, Lipstadt's own account of her experience, which reads like a good courtroom thriller;

---

[6]Emory University, "Holocaust Denial on Trial," http://www.hdot.org/en/trial/transcripts/.

and Richard J. Evans, *Lying about Hitler: History, Holocaust, and the David Irving Trial.*[7] Evans is Professor of Modern History at the University of Cambridge, a specialist on Nazi Germany, and the key expert witness at the Irving trial. He is also a historian who has spent time reflecting on the nature of the discipline, and his account of the trial is as much an exposition and demonstration of the applicability of his own method as it is a story of legal proceedings. I regularly recommend it to postgraduate students who want to be provoked to think about the nature of historical objectivity and meaning.

Probably the single best academic treatment of Holocaust Denial in terms of its historical method is that by Michael Shermer and Alex Grobman, *Denying History: Who Says the Holocaust Never Happened and Why Do They Say It?*[8] This work not only addresses the issue of history versus pseudohistory, but also tackles the philosophical underpinnings of historical narrative, the "free speech" red herrings that are so often thrown up in the debate, and the way in which postmodern posturings that are fun in the classroom have devastating implications (moral and epistemological) for the nature of historical knowledge.

For many, the very notion of HD is absurd, yet it does have a history that dates back almost to the close of the Second World War. Paul Rassinier, a French Socialist and member of the Resistance who had himself been imprisoned in the camps at Dora and Buchenwald, published a number of books, starting with *Le Passage de la Ligne* ("Crossing the Line") in 1948. His collected works were published in one tome, *Debunking the Genocide Myth*, by Noontide Press, an outlet for neo-Nazi works, in 1977. His work essentially argued that the worst treatment in the camps was meted out not by administrators but by the inmates themselves, that eyewitness accounts were no more than embittered gossip, and that what killings did occur were not part of any organized extermination policy authorized from

---

[7]Deborah E. Lipstadt, *History on Trial: My Day in Court with a Holocaust Denier* (New York: Harper Perennial, 2006); Richard J. Evans, *Lying about Hitler: History, Holocaust, and the David Irving Trial* (New York: Basic Books, 2001).
[8]Michael Shermer and Alex Grobman, *Denying History: Who Says the Holocaust Never Happened and Why Do They Say It?* (Berkeley, CA: University of California Press, 2000).

the top but the result of maverick actions by those lower down the chain of command. Of course, what's good for the goose is good for the gander, and so we need to know where Rassinier was coming from in order to understand the biases of his history: these were intimately connected to the fact that he was indeed treated worse by the inmates than he was by the camp guards and apparently wanted to settle old scores after the war. Now, this does not in itself invalidate his account, but given the peculiar strength that an argument for HD coming from an actual inmate has, it is worth noting that his testimony was not as disinterested as it might at first seem.

Strange as Rassinier's claims were, he was only the first of a long stream of writers that continues to the present day: any Internet search on the names Harry Elmer Barnes, Austin J. App, Arthur R. Butz, Fred Leuchter, Robert Faurisson, David Irving, or the word "Holohoax" reveals a world that is thankfully unknown to most, but which takes itself very seriously indeed and loses no opportunity to present itself as representing thoughtful, scholarly, and courageous history. What started as a bizarre and strange testimony from a camp inmate has become a veritable industry.

Basic Strategies: Eyewitness Testimony

Given the apparent mass of documentary evidence in favor of the Holocaust, one mistake that is frequently made by those who seek to oppose it is that HD is not sophisticated. This is not true. Even a glance at the Web sites with which it is associated will show that, at least on the surface, it is in fact very sophisticated. In researching this book, I spent many an unhappy hour on the Web, looking through this material and was frequently taken aback by the rhetorical power so much of it has. Many HD advocates may be self-evidently driven by extreme political philosophies; but its leading advocates are no fools.

A good example of how HD is frequently underestimated was provided by an (in)famous encounter on an American TV show between an advocate of HD and a survivor of the Holocaust (actually an Auschwitz survivor), a meeting that also highlighted some of the strategies used by HD advocates.

During the debate, the Holocaust survivor swore that human beings had been made into soap and lampshades at Auschwitz.[9] Now there is little or no evidence that this was ever the case, and the fact that Michael Shermer, himself on the program, had to correct the lady gave rhetorical power to the HD case as then presented.

The human soap story is, according to Shermer and Grobman, one of the most misunderstood topics in Holocaust research.[10] While there is no evidence that this was ever done on a mass scale and only very limited evidence that it was even tried as an experiment, it is one of those stories that has become stock-in-trade of Holocaust discussions at a popular level. Thus, the fact that it was stated by a Holocaust survivor and swiftly refuted by a reputable Holocaust historian appeared problematic to say the least.

This encounter highlights the limited usefulness of eyewitness testimony. This woman had been in Auschwitz, yet she claimed to have seen soap that never existed. How so? The answer is surely that a combination of time, of constantly hearing accounts of the Holocaust in which lurid tales, some true and some false, played a prominent part, of the tricks of an aging memory, and of the emotional trauma of being up against someone on prime time television who was denying something that had caused her much suffering and presumably taken the lives of many of her loved ones—all these thing combined to make her memory unreliable. It is clear from the transcript that her outbursts were verging on the hysterical, and we can all understand why that would be the case; but this also served to make her testimony less reliable and persuasive.

Of course, one does not have to be a historian to understand the complexities involved in eyewitness testimony. Contrary to popular belief, in the legal world, eyewitness testimony is not the knockout punch that many people think it is. A few years ago, a young man was shot and killed in London by members of the British Special Branch at the end of a brief chase in a London tube (subway) station. He had been under surveil-

---

[9]A verbatim account of the exchange is given in Shermer and Grobman, *Denying History*, 110–14.
[10]Shermer and Grobman, *Denying History*, 114.

lance for a while, suspected of being a terrorist. Tragically, he was simply someone whose visa had expired, which accounted for the fact that he ran away when approached by the police; he had no link to terror groups and no intention of harming anybody.

Now, I remember watching the news reports coming in that day, a number of which included eyewitness testimony from people who claimed to have seen the final moments of the chase and the shooting of the young man. The descriptions given were earnest, detailed, and utterly convincing; and yet, as the dust settled and the facts emerged, it became clear that the "eyewitnesses" had not actually witnessed the shooting at all; all they had seen was the general pandemonium that had gripped the tube station for a few moments; their testimony was nonsense.

So, were these so-called eyewitnesses lying? Were they part of some conspiracy to portray the events of that day in a particular light? Were they consciously trying to put the police and the journalists off the scent, or gain a Warholesque fifteen minutes of fame for themselves? Now, I do not know any of them personally, but I very much doubt that any of these were the case. I suspect they were describing events just as they thought they had seen them; but what they had seen was a scene of total chaos which, on its own, was simply incomprehensible. Then, as the chaos died down, the air around them would have been filled with rumors, interpretations, and statements about what had gone on; these would have provided categories by which they were able to start making sense of what had happened; and then, as they started to give their accounts of what had happened (to compose their little histories of the day, we might say), they offered not simply empirical restatements of the events but rather interpretations of the chaos based on the categories they had imbibed. They genuinely believed their stories, but their stories were fundamentally flawed, if not completely wrong at many points.

Of course, most readers of this book will be able to think of analogous moments in their own lives when they have remembered an event one way and found out that it must have happened another way. Often this can be related to details of chronology; at other times it can be related to major events or happenings. To be aware of this, and thus of the limitations of eyewitness and memory testimony, is an important step on the path to being a critical historian. Yet the problems with eyewitness testimony do not end with the faultiness of human memory or the misleading results of reading events through the grid of certain categories. The whole genre of autobiographical testimony is subject to the problems of self-interest: when individuals recount events or actions from their past, they usually do so with particular agendas or axes to grind. As Churchill once commented, "History will be kind to me, for I intend to write it." At least he was honest; for which person, writing about events in which they were involved or by which they were impacted, will not make sure that their role or involvement is presented in the manner which they desire?

What was significant on the TV encounter was the language the HD advocate immediately used about the woman's statement: he referred to it as a lie, not necessarily implying that she was consciously lying, but that she had believed a lie. Shermer countered by saying that it was not a lie but a mistake. This is a crucial difference. A lie is intentional, and, as such, its perpetrator or originator is deliberately stating something he knows to be an untruth. By the time this woman repeated the human soap story, it was not for her a lie; rather, it was a mistake, and mistakes can be corrected by examination of evidence, argument, and the subsequent refining of knowledge that takes place. To cast the whole thing as a lie, as the HD advocate did, is immediately to bring that whiff of conspiracy and suspicion of active suppression of the truth into play, something that often works well in a society with an insatiable appetite for conspiracy as a means of alleviating the mundane, whether with reference to the Holocaust or the death of Michael Jackson. The truth is too often thought to be out there, but being actively covered up by the powers that be.

Returning to the specific issue of eyewitness testimony, the question is, in light of the above, how do we as historians evaluate its usefulness as historical evidence? The answer is that we need to be careful and critical of eyewitness testimony, whether it is documented in the immediate aftermath of events (as in the case of the London police shooting) or decades after the events (as in the Holocaust survivor on the television show). It is useful, not least for adding some drama to our work, but it has distinct limitations, and so the historian must take these into account when putting together a narrative explanation of the past.

The fact is, however, that we do not depend for our understanding of the past, either entirely or predominantly, on eyewitness testimony. There are certain genres of history, such as oral history, that do offer insights into the past, particularly of those whose thoughts and experiences are typically ignored by mainstream historical narratives (generally, the poor); but the grand narratives of history and the most solid historical assertions cannot be built exclusively on such testimony. Instead, historians typically bring eyewitness testimony into relation with other historical artifacts in order to establish what happened and when it happened.

Thus, for example, in the shooting of the man on the London Underground, eyewitness testimonies were no doubt collected from all who saw—or thought they saw—what happened that day. But far more important would have been empirical evidence such as the position of the body, the number, type, and angles of the bullets used to kill him, and any video footage that might have been available from security cameras. Now, it is *possible* that any of this evidence could have been manipulated, but, in the absence of compelling reasons for, or evidence of, such tampering, it inevitably plays a significant role in assessing the validity of any eyewitness statements. Indeed, no doubt the empirical evidence was used by the investigating officers to set certain parameters by which the veracity and reliability of the eyewitness testimony could be tested. If somebody, for example, claimed to have heard a submachine firing repeat rounds for thirty seconds, but the only bullets recovered at the scene numbered half a dozen and were all fired from a single police revolver, then clearly the testimony has to be discounted until such time as the missing submachine bullets, not to mention the missing submachine gun, should turn up.

All this is to say that, when a survivor of the Holocaust appears on an American television show and makes a statement that is demonstrably false, such as having seen human soap at Auschwitz, it may well be shocking but it does not make a significant dent in the arguments for the historical reality of the Holocaust. Of course, for the average person in the studio or television audience, the error is disturbing and no doubt serves to start raising questions in the person's mind about the reliability of the standard Holocaust narratives; but in the context of serious history, it is of little account. The narratives of the Holocaust are not built exclusively, or even primarily, on eyewitness recollections given more than forty years after the events described. Yet, just for the record, it is worth noting that this is precisely how Holocaust Denial operates: it creates doubts in the overall narrative by highlighting myriad inconsistencies or errors in the minor details of the evidence, as if the cumulative effect of such is sufficient to overthrow the edifice as a whole. In history, however, failure to achieve precision and accuracy on a host of minor points does not mean that the larger claims of a particular historical narrative are negotiable, or that the narrative is merely one equally valid version among many, or that it is epistemologically ungrounded. One eyewitness might remember Napoleon wearing a blue coat at Waterloo, another a red one, but the conflict in testimony does not impinge upon the fact of the battle itself. Thus, the reality of the Holocaust can be established on grounds other than that of eyewitness testimony; and, indeed, the Holocaust deniers know this and thus have spent much time and money trying to shatter the credibility of other evidence.

Basic Strategies: Scientific Evidence

We know that the survivor of Auschwitz was probably mistaken in her claims that she had seen soap and lampshades made from human beings at Auschwitz because there is no evidence, documentary or otherwise, that such things took place at the camp. But what about gas chambers? Anyone who knows anything about the Holocaust knows that Auschwitz, while not strictly a death camp designed with the sole purpose of executing everybody who was delivered to the gates, was yet the scene of mass murder on a technological scale that is hard to comprehend. Indeed, the difficulty of believing the sheer figures involved has not gone unnoticed by many advocates of Holocaust Denial. Unlike the means used for soap production, of course, the gas chambers and crematoria remain as archaeological artifacts, and are proof positive that such mass murder took place.

Or are they? One of the major planks of Holocaust Denial over the past decades has been the attempt to refute the scientific evidence of the gas chambers, to make the case that these buildings need to be understood as fulfilling a different purpose to that which is ascribed to them in the standard histories of the camp.

Central to this exercise has been the so-called Leuchter Report, written by Fred Leuchter in 1989. Its full title is *The Leuchter Report: An Engineering Report on the Alleged Execution Chambers at Auschwitz, Birkenau, and Majdanek, Poland.* The report appears to have been commissioned by Ernst Zündel, a Holocaust denier who was at the time on trial for his views in Canada. In this report, Leuchter makes a series of claims that would seem, on the surface, to do serious damage to the idea that there were gas chambers at Auschwitz which had been used for mass murder.

First, he claims that the Nazis who dropped the gas pellets through the holes in the roof of the chambers would themselves have been killed by the gas they were releasing on their hapless victims, thus, they could not have done so. Second, he claims that that the traces of Zyklon-B, the deadly gas used for the mass executions, was stronger in the delousing chambers than in the execution chambers, a finding that made no sense on the grounds that the killing of millions of people would have required almost continual operation of the chambers. Third, he claims that use of Zyklon-B in proximity to the crematoria was highly dangerous and would have caused an explosion.

At first glance these are disturbing claims, especially given the apparently scientific form in which they are articulated; and, like the incorrect eyewitness testimony of the Auschwitz survivor, they might well shake the confidence of the casual nonhistorian in the received wisdom about the Holocaust. But the historian must stop at this point and ask questions about the interpretation which Leuchter is placing upon the evidence. His claims may appear to be scientific and thus somewhat compelling, but we need to ask if they are quite as compelling as is claimed by inquiring as to whether there are not other, more likely explanations for the phenomena under discussion.

As to the first claim, it is surely an obvious point that it took a few minutes for the Zyklon-B pellets to break down and for the deadly gas to spread, presumably from the ground upward. Thus, if the pellets were dropped by the Nazis into the chambers through the holes in the roof, then as long as the Nazis closed the vents and exited from the roof area, they would not have been affected by the gas. To claim that they would all have died and thus that it was too risky a procedure is nonsense. We might say that only very stupid Nazis would have died in this process. Of course, one might object that somebody still had to check the chambers to see if the gas had done its deadly work; but within the camp structure certain inmates were employed as what were known as "Sonderkommandos" who would be used to do precisely this kind of dirty, dangerous work. Because they were simply inmates, the camp authorities cared nothing for their safety, and they had no choice but to do as they were told. They could easily be sent in to check the chambers, and if they died, so what?[11]

Thus, an apparently plausible criticism of the gas chamber thesis is, on careful examination, somewhat less convincing. We see from this the importance of connecting the historical claim with a reconstruction of what was actually happening. Once we understand how the gas dispersed after the pellets were dropped through holes in the roof of the chambers, the claim that it would have been suicide for SS guards to have been involved at that stage of the operation becomes implausible; and once we understand something of the way in which the camps were administered, and that a group of dispensable workers, the Sonderkommandos, were available to do the highly dangerous work of checking the chambers after the executions, the final part of Leuchter's first claim disappears. Thus, the historian can assess Leuchter's claim by setting it in the context of the physical design of the gas chambers and the organization of the camp personnel. Once this is done, Leuchter's interpretation becomes less than compelling.

The second claim, that based on the varying strengths of gas residue found in the walls of the execution chambers and delousing chambers

---

[11]These precise points were made by the judge when he challenged Leuchter at the Zündel trial, and Leuchter conceded them: see Shermer and Grobman, *Denying History*, 130.

respectively, has particular power, at least at first glance. Part of this is surely the result of the culture in which we live, where the results of scientific tests are regarded as possessing great persuasive power on the grounds that they are seen as more objective than, say, eyewitness testimony. Now, there is a whole trajectory of thought in the contemporary world that has seriously questioned the objectivity of science, and the idea that science is a strictly neutral exercise no longer enjoys widespread currency. But even allowing for the fact that science is perhaps not as clean and precise as once thought, scientific results still have power, and deservedly so. Think, for example, of the many times in the last decade that DNA evidence has been used to overturn that of eyewitnesses. If I remember seeing Mr. Smith beating up Mr. Jones on the corner of the street, but DNA evidence indicates that it was actually Mr. Brown, a person of similar build, whose fists were pummeling the victim, then guess what? The jury is going to acquit Mr. Smith, and the police will charge Mr. Brown with the crime. Thus, when a man like Leuchter comes along and claims that the scientific evidence does not sustain claims about gas chambers being used for executions, most of us are inclined to sit up and take notice. This is far more serious than the faulty memories of a distressed survivor of Auschwitz.

In fact, however, Leuchter's second point is not as strong as it appears to be; it is dressed up in the rhetoric of science, but on closer inspection it actually lacks the very scientific basis which it claims for itself. First, nobody has ever claimed that six million people were executed in a single gas chamber. That would be ridiculous and easy to refute. Typically, Holocaust historians estimate that a third to a half of the dead died from other causes: disease, overwork, starvation, firing squads and, at an earlier point in the process, vans with engines pumping exhaust fumes into the hold. So the idea that the gas chamber at Auschwitz would have needed to be running flat out, nearly all day every day, is incorrect. Whatever gas residue there would have been should not be based on estimates that assume such activity. This is the classic straw man strategy: misrepresent the position against which one is arguing, and thereby give your own position apparent compelling strength.

Second, the contrast in residue between the gas chambers and the delousing units is explicable on the basis of the different physiological responses of human beings and lice to Zyklon-B. Human beings breathe the poison gas in through their lungs, absorb it rapidly, and die within a couple of minutes. Once this had been done at Auschwitz, the gas would be released from the chambers and the bodies taken off to the crematorium. In other words, there would have been minimal time for any residue to build up within the walls. Lice, however, take much longer to die from Zyklon-B, and so the process for delousing clothes would take between twelve and eighteen hours. In other words, the gas would have remained in the delousing chambers for extended periods of time, allowing for a much greater concentration of the poison to accumulate within the walls of the chamber.

Once these factors are taken into account, the disturbing disparity in Zyklon-B residue between death chambers and delousing chambers seems not so damaging to the traditional thesis. Leuchter's observation has a specious shock value and plausibility, but on closer inspection, the results are entirely consistent with what one would expect to find if the received interpretation is indeed the correct one. Again, as historians, we see the need to ask the right questions about the evidence and the interpretation being offered; and, dare I say, we also see the need to understand how sophisticated and interdisciplinary the discipline of history is. On this single point alone, a knowledge both of the actual claims being made by Holocaust historians and of the comparative physiologies of human beings and lice is crucial for seeing through Leuchter's argument.

Yet there is a further damaging factor to take into account at this point, and that relates to the overall accuracy of traces of Zyklon-B that can be found in the walls of the various chambers. The gas chambers at Auschwitz were destroyed by the Nazis as the Russians pushed through Poland in 1944. That which stands there today is a reconstruction; all that remains of the originals is a pile of rubble. As such, the material that made up the inner walls of the chambers has been exposed to wind, rain, sun, and snow for decades. When Leuchter put together his report in the late eighties, this had been the case for nearly half a century. The question, therefore, of how this weather damage would have distorted the residue results (and, indeed, how Leuchter knew which pieces of brick were from the gas chamber lining) is a pressing one. The lack of a scientific control, to which the Auschwitz bricks could be compared, makes the results less than scientific at best; and Leuchter and others failed to mention the fact that their samples were taken from a reconstructed gas chamber, made up of bricks from the original chamber and from other buildings. The claims to scientific analyses are built upon very unscientific methods.[12]

Leuchter's third point, that the proximity of the gas chambers to the crematoria made explosions inevitable, is another specious claim. For a start, the crematoria were separate, self-contained units, and the flames they generated were enclosed within them, not open. One is inclined to ask, how many crematoria are there, anywhere in the world, where the flames are in the open air? The Auschwitz crematoria were scarcely typical in a number of ways, but archaeological and photographic evidence suggests they were sealed, brick structures; and that makes perfect sense if the Nazis did not want to blow the camp sky high. No other hypothesis is needed to explain the evidence at this point. In addition, as Shermer and Grobman point out, it requires only three hundred parts per million of Zyklon-B to kill a human being; to cause an explosion requires fifty-six thousand parts per million. That is a significant difference.[13]

We have now looked at two aspects of the HD case: the focus on problems with eyewitness testimony, designed to shake confidence in the eyewitness record; and the scientific report of Fred Leuchter, which, ironically, is susceptible to devastating critique based on its own stated methods, namely, those of modern science. This debunking of the debunkers, however, does not prove that the Holocaust happened; it merely demonstrates the insufficiency of the arguments mounted against the orthodox proponents of Holocaust history. Before turning to positive evidence for the Holocaust, however, it is worth reflecting at least briefly on one further aspect of the culture of HD which is of wider signifi-

---

[12] Shermer and Grobman, *Denying History*, 132.
[13] Ibid., 131.

cance for those engaged in the discipline of history. This is what I call "the aesthetic fallacy."

The Aesthetic Fallacy

Put simply, the aesthetic fallacy is the belief that if it looks convincing, it is convincing; or, to refine it slightly, if it looks scholarly, then, agree or disagree with it, it is scholarly and must be taken seriously and allowed a place at the scholarly table. Unlike other classic fallacies—intentional, root, reification, anachronism, etc.—the aesthetic fallacy is not so much a fallacy of the author or historian as a fallacy of the reader. It is not the historian who makes the mistake; indeed, he may well have intentionally written in such a way as to lead to the aesthetic fallacy. It is the reader who is duped by the form of what she reads into assuming the arguments presented are much stronger than they really are.

In my own academic experience, the most obvious example of this relates to my own time as a PhD student in the late eighties. My class at secondary (high) school was very much one which represented educational transition. I was the last person who pursued Latin to Advanced Level, and a member of the last year for whom computing was not part of the central curriculum. The result was that I went through undergraduate studies and my first year of doctoral work without touching the keyboard of a word processor. It may be inconceivable to a generation raised on PCs, Macs, and iPods, but I was one of those dinosaurs who actually wrote out class notes and essays with a pen and paper (and who, incidentally, thought the special effects of Ray Harryhausen in films like *Jason and the Argonauts* were the most convincing things ever).

It was in my second year of doctoral studies that my supervisor kindly allowed me to use his office and computer when he was away. I think he had reached the point of despair with regard to my handwritten, barely legible papers and simply wanted something that was easier to read. Thus, I began to type up and print out my thoughts. I suspect it is hard for today's student to understand the stunning effect of seeing one's prose printed in a decent font for the first time, but believe me, the experience was a psychological watershed. Suddenly my writing seemed more coherent, my arguments more convincing, and, with the addition of footnotes, my papers more scholarly and compelling. Of course, I am sure that the use of a word processor did change my style somewhat—the ability to use footnotes obviously had an impact, as did the ease with which corrections could be made and great chunks of text shuffled around and rearranged; but what was significant was that it was the *look* of my papers that made them seem more serious rather than any quality intrinsic to the argument or the research.

Aesthetics are all-important, from the choice of laptop to the design of kitchens to the covers of books. Anyone who says differently is talking nonsense: we all like things that are not simply functional but also look good, and there is nothing wrong with that. But we must always be on our guard against confusing functionality with appearance. If I buy a cool looking computer that does not actually work, then I have wasted my money; having said that, a computer that works but is ugly in design is less likely to be purchased than an attractive counterpart.

I am guessing that few, if any, will have any problem with what I have said above, and we can surely extend the argument a little without much controversy. Take politics: it is not enough to make a good argument these days; indeed, good arguments, because they are often prolix, complex, and subtle, are frequently the last thing you actually need as a politician. A sound bite, a suntan, a nice smile, and a sharp suit are more use than the ability to parse the nature of the gross domestic product, talk authoritatively about credit balances, or outline the subtleties of foreign policy. Again, few thoughtful people, reflecting on the power of the televisual media, would object to such a claim.

What I want to suggest now, however, is that aesthetics are also important in the scholarly world. As noted above, seeing my own immature scribblings in twelve-point Times New Roman was a revolutionary experience; I never thought of my writing in quite the same way again. Suddenly, my prose was more compelling and persuasive than I had ever dared imagine. Aesthetics made a big difference; the very appearance of my words in print form gave plausibility to my work. And what was true of me as a humble postgraduate is even more true of the scholarly world in general. I suspect, indeed, that aesthetics impacts most disciplines; it certainly does so with regard to the practice of history, and this is something of which the HD advocates are well aware.

We have already seen a form of this in the scientific arguments of Leuchter. On close examination, we can easily see that his method is so flawed that it is not really scientific at all, but it has all the appearance of being scientific. He uses all the right words, even down to his claim in the title that he is an engineer. In fact, he is not; he is a designer of execution machines. Indeed, he has been barred from using the title "engineer" with reference to himself because of his lack of formal qualifications.[14] The title gave him weight and plausibility; he presumably hoped that it would provide him with the credibility to have a seat at the table and be taken seriously in discussions. One could say that the scientific *form* of his writing, or perhaps better (though slightly more pretentiously), the scientific *aesthetics* of his work gave his arguments credibility. For this reason, I am always suspicious of books that print "PhD" on the cover after the author's name. Why do they need to do this? The person has written a book, so surely her competence can be judged by the volume's contents? Perhaps, after all, many books are judged at least somewhat by their covers as well as what is printed on the inside.

In fact, the aesthetic fallacy, as deployed by HD advocates, is not restricted to Leuchter and his report. Central to HD has been the role of an organization known as the Institute for Historical Review. My own interest in HD was first aroused when a Jewish colleague at the University of Nottingham alerted me to their Web page (www.ihr.org). The Institute was founded by two figures of the British and American anti-Semitic far right, David McCalden and Willis Carto, respectively. It is an interesting organization because of the way in which it seeks to garner credibility for its cause by the careful use of aesthetics. For example, its Web page is an interesting mix of current news stories and links to serious, mainstream media outlets. The impression given is one of a general concern for world

---

[14]Ibid., 130.

affairs. But spend any time on the site and it becomes clear that many of the stories focus on the Middle East, or Israeli oppression of Palestinians, or, closer to home, activities of Jewish lawyers and politicians. Dig deeper, and one finds HD material on the sidebar and through various links provided. The approach is clever: produce a mainstream aesthetic that almost imperceptibly guides the reader toward HD material and juxtapose, say, an article advocating HD with a link to a serious news magazine like *The Economist*, and an atmosphere of credibility pervades the site, no matter how peculiar some of the views expressed. Even the name of the institute plays to aesthetic sensibilities: the use of the word "review" in the title inspires thoughts of a scholarly, critical spirit and of those who are willing to examine any received orthodoxy in light of the evidence. This kind of sentiment is reinforced by the rhetoric of some of the articles that typically describe opposition to HD as "political correctness" and that characterize HD advocates as the brave few, speaking up against a conspiratorial consensus (often driven by Jews and the pro-Israel lobby).

A good example of this is provided by an article by one Robin Davis, entitled, "Holocaust Denial and Uncomfortable Truths."[15] The article begins as follows:

> It has always been those few who can see through the political correctness and hypocrisy of popular attitudes who are considered dangerous.
>
> "Holocaust denial laws" are now in place in about a dozen countries. Defenders of these laws claim that the expression of unconventional views about the Jewish genocide is "hate speech" and "incitement to violence" and therefore must be suppressed.
>
> But history shows the greatest purveyors of lies, hatred and incitement to violence are those with the power to spread their poison by manipulating popular opinion via the control or complicity of the mass media. Through a purposefully constructed lens of political correctness the despicable becomes normal. It is by this insidious process that tyrants make it normal and accept-

---

[15]Robin Davis, "Holocaust Denial and Uncomfortable Truths" linked from Institute for Historical Review, www.ihr.org to Countercurrents.org, http://www.countercurrents.org/davis060609.htm (accessed July 8, 2009).

able to murder those whom they consider threatening or inferior. We have only to turn on the television to see that process at work.

It is not the unpopular views we should fear but the popular.

When the suppression of free speech serves no purpose other than to silence unconventional opinions we should be alarmed. We should be even more alarmed when to question oppressive laws is to risk vilification, in this case by the smear of "Holocaust denier" and "anti-Semite".

Appropriation of the term "The Holocaust" to the Nazi extermination of the Jews minimises the significance of other genocides, including those that are happening right now. Should these crimes also be closed to opinions that question the accuracy of the official "truth"?

There you have it: HD advocates are champions of the truth and of free speech; they are opponents of those in power who are trying to suppress the truth; and they are the real champions of human rights in their refusal to relativize other genocides by making the Holocaust exceptional. The game is clear: to play to the buzz words of the modern world (free speech), to aim ammunition at targets of popular mistrust (those with power), and to pull at the emotional heartstrings by pointing to other genocides.

It is thus important to notice two things about this passage. First, it is entirely rhetorical; it contains no substantial argumentation about evidence whatsoever but is designed rather to divert the reader to issues of, for want of a better word, taste, and to win immediate sympathy for the case that is about to be made. He could be arguing on behalf of the people who think the moon is made of cream cheese or who think that Elvis is alive and well and working in a supermarket in Michigan; the same points about freedom of speech, unnamed power brokers, and conspiratorial attempts to suppress the truth could still be made. In other words, this passage is designed merely to pull on the heartstrings and to sow doubt in the mind of the reader about received wisdom. It is an aesthetic argument that relies on its form and its choice of words and clichés for its power.

Second, notice how successful it is. Few, if any, can read this passage and not feel the little hairs of doubt starting to stick up on the back of their necks. But why? There are no evidential arguments here, no set of logically connected and evidentially verified statements designed to establish a specific historical proposition. This is not history; it is rhetorical flourish with mischievous intent. To make the argument compelling in any scholarly sense, we need to see evidence of the alleged conspiracy to silence these heroes of truth. We need argument, not just high sounding phrases, but the truth is that we live in a culture where certain phrases, images, and ideas have emotional power, and this writer plays to a number of them. It is a salutary reminder that, while history should not be boring, we need to take care not to fall prey to the aesthetic fallacy.

Before moving on, it is worth commenting briefly on the writer's final point, as this is one which can be discussed in terms other than its rhetorical power. We might even extend his argument that the Holocaust is not exceptional by noting that it is not the only genocide to have attracted "deniers": the 1915 massacre of Armenians by the Turks has also been questioned by some. As to its exceptionalism, there is a sense in which the Holocaust can be seen as one instance of the larger phenomenon of ethnic slaughter, under which one could add the Armenian massacre, the Rape of Nanking, and the more recent tragic events in the Balkans and Africa. Yet at another level it is exceptional for its planning and organization, its use of technology, its elaborate ideological and philosophical motivation, and for the fact that it was given birth by a nation that was arguably the most culturally advanced in Europe at the time and where the primary ethnic minority that was its target, the Jews, had been extremely well-integrated into society.

All of this playing to the gallery again serves to win the sympathy of the audience and to enhance credibility, but, as anyone familiar with the anti-HD literature knows, it is specious at best. Mainstream historians oppose HD not because it is politically incorrect or even because it is advocated by people allied to some of the creepiest political creeds; rather, they oppose it because it is bad history that fails by any canons of good history one might care to suggest.

More than in the clever use of rhetoric and media-savvy Web page construction, the aesthetic subterfuge can be seen in the primary print organ used by the IHR for spreading its views: the *Journal of Historical Review*, which was published between 1980 and 2002. Anybody familiar with the practices and idioms of academic disciplines will know that journals have been central to the enterprise. The library of my institution spends a significant part of its budget on subscription to academic journals and, like most teachers in higher education, I subscribe to a couple myself and on occasion have published articles in the same. They typically have an editor and an editorial board of named scholars, and publish only what is called peer reviewed material, that is, material which has been read by qualified people in the field who have found it to reach the requisite academic standards. Such journals are, to put it bluntly, usually very boring in appearance and rather dry in content; but that, strange to tell, is the aesthetic that one therefore comes to expect with such things. Boring and dry in appearance has come to imply scholarly and reliable in content.

Thus, the production of a journal by an organization such as the IHR was a brilliant move, and theirs did indeed conform to the standard academic protocols in terms of appearance: it had all the look of a serious journal, and it contained a smattering of articles not targeted directly at advocating HD as well as the occasional piece even written by opponents of HD. Thus, the mix of HD and other interests served to give the appearance that the journal had no specific agenda beyond finding its way to real history and the truth.

The significance of this for those pursuing the historian's craft but who have no interest in the arcane weirdness of HD is simply this: the historian needs to be aware of the power of aesthetics when it comes to assessing evidence and argument. As Leuchter described himself as an engineer and thus gave his report an aesthetic of scientific credibility, so groups like the IHR have clothed themselves with the idioms and aesthetics of scholarship and have pressed the rhetorical hot buttons of the wider culture in order to sow doubts about the received consensus and inspire thoughts of conspiratorial efforts to suppress the truth. They hope to gain a foothold in the discussion that at least grants a legitimacy to their view and thus relativizes all the evidence against their position. As the debate between intentionalists and functionalists can be seen to be between two opposed camps which yet answer to the same canons of historical method and truth, so the HD advocates aspire to sit at the same table, and aesthetics is an important part of the plan to find their way there. This is why we must be careful to judge any argument not so much by the type of font used or the paper on which it is printed, as by the cogency of its case and the careful use of sources. A large number of impressive footnotes does not a true case make. Sources need to be checked, counterpositions need to be taken into consideration. Even in refuting an absurdity such as HD this is the case: once the sources are examined, the case for HD vanishes like the morning mist.

The Use of Positive Evidence

Thus far in this chapter we have reflected on aspects of historical method by looking at the shortcomings of HD: we have seen that, disturbing as it may be on first encounter, the incoherence of eyewitness testimony does not mean the Holocaust did not happen, given that eyewitness testimony is notoriously unreliable; rather, it means simply that we must not build our case for historical truth exclusively on eyewitnesses or, if we have to do so, we should be aware of the provisional nature and the limitations of such a case. Second, we have seen that evidence presented as scientific can often fall far below scientific standards. When scientific evidence is used and interpreted, we need to ask critical questions, such as: What is the nature of this scientific evidence? How was it obtained? Are there any available controls by which to judge the evidence? Is this proposed interpretation the most likely to be true? Finally, we noted the importance of being aware of how manipulative the form, or aesthetics, of an argument can be: put it in a nice typeface or what looks like a reputable journal or a book from a reputable publisher, or trumpet the author as some kind of professionally recognized expert in a field, and you can make almost any case more powerful and persuasive than it might otherwise have been.

The question now arises, "Where do we go from here? You have shown me the shortcomings in the approach of HD, but can you make a positive case that there is such a thing as real history, that not all narratives of the Holocaust, for example, are equally valid, that there is a fundamental difference between the range of opinions embraced by the intentionalist/functionalist debate and those included under the rubric of HD?"

In some senses, this is the key question. Radical postmodern relativists who reduce all history to tropes or aesthetics and who want to debunk the claims of any approach to the past as being "more true" than any other often do so on ethical grounds: the white heterosexual male history must be dethroned because it helps to perpetuate the oppression of the Other, whether the Other is women, blacks, gays, etc.[16] This is done primarily by way of discounting the referentiality of historical narrative either as irrelevant or simply inaccessible, and by emphasizing rather the aesthetics of narrative construction. In other words, it is the *way* the story is told that is crucial, not so much whether or how the story corresponds to what actually happened. Ironically, of course, the denial or dismissal of the importance or possibility of referentiality in historical writing is the very move that might prevent Holocaust writing from being ethical, because it opens the way for HD, or at least prevents a cogent response to the same; and, as a historian, I would argue there is nothing ethically admirable about those who deny the reality of the Holocaust.

Now, we need to be clear that historians always have some kind of moral or ethical agenda that shapes the way they construct and present their narratives. In the fourth century, the *Life of Anthony*, popularly ascribed to the great bishop of Alexandria, Athanasius, is a wonderful story of how a young man gives up his wealthy life of comfort and heads into the desert to become an Anchorite (a kind of solo monk, or hermit). During his life he performs various miracles: for example, he crosses the Arsenoitic Canal and is not harmed by the crocodiles who dwell there. Given the close connection between crocodiles and certain Egyptian deities, the writer is making the point that Athanasius's God is stronger than those of the pagan culture around him. Did the event really happen? Well, we do not know

---

[16]Interestingly enough, the Other is rarely defined by such postmoderns in terms with which the middle-class intelligentsia would be uncomfortable: members of the Ku Klux Klan, Holocaust deniers, serial killers, and collectors of other people's toenail clippings would all seem to have first-class claims to having been marginalized and written out of the dominant narratives of this world; but none, so far as I know, enjoys the support of a significant postmodern lobby group.

as we only have the writer's word for it; but, at another level, it does not really matter since the point is really a didactic one—that the Christian God is sovereign and better than the other gods out there—rather than a historical one—that Anthony was not eaten by crocodiles. The matter of historical fact is unverifiable and not that important to the way the story was intended or functions.

There are plenty of other examples of which one could think. The famous *Newgate Calendar* of the eighteenth and nineteenth centuries was a collection of stories of the crimes and misdemeanors of various villains who invariably came to sticky ends. The book was historical in the sense that the main characters really existed, really committed crimes, and really came to bad ends; but the stories were told in sensational ways and designed to instill fear and dread in the children to whom they were meant to be read as warnings of the bad ends that inevitably come to those who choose to walk in paths of unrighteousness. The basic pattern is something like this: little Richard was rude to his parents; eventually he became highwayman Dick Turpin, did a lot of very illegal things, and was hanged by the neck for his trouble. Again, the moral agendas of the writers shaped the way the stories were told and quite probably led to embellishments of the basic storyline that could not be verified but which were nonetheless essential to the purpose of the work.

With postmodernists claiming that texts have no fixed meaning, the door now seems to be open to seeing all texts as having an infinite number of potentially irreconcilable interpretations; all that is left, at this point, all that really matters, are the aesthetics and the ethics of interpretation. While this in itself raises a host of philosophical questions about what exactly constitutes ethics in a postmodern world which, thankfully, I have neither the time nor the competence to address here, it does pose the problematic question once again of, is there good history, is there bad history, and how do we tell the difference? And, in the case of the Holocaust, the stakes would seem to be extremely high, given the massive impact it had on countless individual lives and how it has shaped world politics since 1945 and thus continues to affect generations who were then unborn.

At this point, we need to make a distinction between historical theories (Marxism and the like) and historical method. Some would reject this distinction, and I am certainly willing to concede that where method ends and theory begins can be a somewhat gray area, but that does not mean the distinction cannot be made. I grew up by the River Severn. At the estuary, it was unclear to me where the Severn ended and the Atlantic Ocean began; but I knew that it was not the River Severn which lapped against the coast of Florida. Criticizing the postmodern historian Keith Jenkins (who spends more time writing *about* history than actually *doing* history, which is always a bad sign), Richard J. Evans says this:

> Keith Jenkins has argued that historical method does not lead to historical truth. But in saying this, he confuses theory and method. Historical method is not what he says it is—feminist, neo-Marxist, structuralist, *Annaliste*, Weberian or whatever. These things are *theories*. Historical *method* is based on the rules of verification laid down by Ranke and elaborated in numerous ways since his time. It is common to all historians working in all these various theoretical modes, as a glance at their heavily footnoted works will easily show. Even major methodological differences, for example between cliometricians churning quantitative data through their computers, intellectual historians engaged in a close reading of a small number of texts, or medieval historians deciphering archaeological finds, still fade into the background in comparison with the shared duty of "getting it right"—of copying out and punching in the figures accurately, of verifying the wording and authorship of the text, of reporting the correct location of each find in the dig. It is not true to say that historians are "not too concerned about discrete facts." On the contrary, whatever the criteria for the facts' selection, the vast majority of the historians' efforts are devoted to ascertaining them and establishing them as firmly as possible in the light of the historical evidence. Even Jenkins uses footnotes.[17]

Evans point is important, and goes a long way to explaining why good historians can appreciate and interact with others who operate from dif-

---

[17]Richard J. Evans, *In Defence of History* (London: Granta, 1997), 127. Interestingly enough, as noted above, Evans went on to be an expert witness for the defense in the Irving-Lipstadt trial.

ferent theoretical positions. I can read feminist, Marxist, and structuralist works and find them helpful and, indeed, where necessary challenge their findings because, by and large, good historians in these fields are committed to the same kind of methods of verification that I use. While those with different ideological frameworks may well disagree over whether some artifacts constitute evidence, or over the relative importance to be ascribed to certain mutually agreed pieces of evidence, there is in practice, if not total agreement, then at least substantial agreement among historians over what is and is not relevant. For example, the study of seventeenth-century England has been pursued by hard empiricists, Marxists, feminists, and others; and all the representatives of these different groups demonstrate a high degree of agreement in what is and is not relevant evidence for their work. None, to my knowledge, thinks that pottery discovered in Tutankhamen's tomb in the early twentieth century is at all relevant to what happened in England in the seventeenth; and all would agree that pamphlets written by members of the Long Parliament are indeed of interest and importance in some measure to understanding their chosen period. They may differ in how important they see these pamphlets to be, and they may disagree over how they should be interpreted, but they all agree they are relevant to their work in a way that Egyptian potsherds are not.

The simple point is that, for all the postmodern rhetoric, there is a referentiality in the historical task that is intimately connected to evidence. For example, if I have a bus ticket receipt for London resident Mrs. Smith on a certain day in 1926, then I can agree with feminist and Marxist colleagues that Mrs. Smith bought a ticket on that day for that destination. We might disagree on *why* she did it: was she travelling to take part in some element of the General Strike? Was she meeting with a secret group of radical feminists? Was she catching the bus because she belonged to a certain social class that prevented her from having the economic means to own a car? Or did she like riding the bus and simply wanted to visit her grandchildren? All of these are possible interpretations of the action, and may or may not be verifiable or falsifiable depending on what other evidence is available (such as a diary entry by Mrs. Smith or a letter of thanks from a grandchild). But the fact of the ticket purchase is not in doubt, unless we want to weave an elaborate conspiracy theory about a clandestine group of bus ticket forgers who were trying to subvert the historical record by flooding the world with counterfeits; and, unless there is more evidence for this latter notion than the former, as good historians there is no doubt where we should take our stand.

This goes to the heart of the postmodern idea that texts have no fixed meaning. First, it is unlikely that any historian has ever believed that any text—or, perhaps better, historical event or evidence—has ever had one solitary fixed meaning. Take Shakespeare's plays, for example. Has anyone ever thought that they meant just one thing or had significance in only one sense? Can they not be studied as artifacts of the development of stage drama? Of blank verse? Of editorial procedures? As windows into aspects of Elizabethan and Jacobean culture? As examples of the reception of historical narratives into dramatic forms? Etc., etc., etc. But this does not mean they can mean anything, or be seen as significant for everything. There may be an infinite number of books that can be written about them, every one subtly different from every other one, and each using standard approaches to reading, verification, etc. But these readings take place within a frame of reference that is itself limited by certain intrinsic qualities of the text. You cannot, for example, use Shakespeare's *Othello* as a guide for brain surgery. At least, if your brain surgeon tells you that that is where he obtained his knowledge of surgical procedure, I would strongly recommend you ask for a second opinion.

Given this, we can turn our attention back to the Holocaust. Is denial of the Holocaust a legitimate interpretation of the facts of the case? In other words, does it give an account, albeit a provisional and limited one, of the Holocaust that is consistent with the actual historical artifacts? It is true that all facts are interpreted facts, that all historical narratives offer interpretations of the evidence; but it is also true that interpretations can be tested by the evidence and, if shown wanting, they must be modified accordingly or even abandoned.

So far, we have shown that eyewitness testimony cannot be relied upon in itself to support a historical claim in any rock solid manner. Yet the human soap incident, even as it shatters confidence in eyewitness testimony, still gives us an instructive example of how good historical method works: we know that the woman's claim to have seen human soap manufactured at the camp is unreliable and should be treated with skepticism because there is no other evidence of such which would corroborate or support her story. There are no remains of any soap factory on the site and no evidence to suggest it was carefully eradicated; there are no records of such soap production or receipts for delivery of the means for carrying out such production; and there are no corroborative testimonies that would lead us to suspect that the lack of archaeological and paper evidence is at all misleading.

As this small example of historical reasoning shows, Holocaust historians build their case for its reality on a variety of different sources that they use to corroborate each other and thus to establish what happened. Of course, there are eyewitness accounts and contemporary reports that form part of this evidence, and that not just from victims but also from Nazi perpetrators. For example, the Reichsführer-SS Heinrich Himmler, the man with overall control of the Final Solution, had a masseur who wrote about the stomach upsets his boss would suffer after witnessing executions at the camps; Rudolf Höss, the commandant of Auschwitz, also wrote a memoir while in prison awaiting execution after the end of the war, in which he outlined his life and activities at Auschwitz; and there is, of course, the trial of Adolf Eichmann, made famous by Hannah Arendt in her book *Eichmann on Jerusalem: A Report in the Banality of Evil*, where the defendant's testimony was made that much more chilling not by the fact that it was coerced from him under duress but by the fact that he really did not seem to think that he had done anything significantly wrong.[18] Let me stress once again: this evidence is not decisive, and, as we know, such eyewitness accounts can prove to be very unreliable if not sometimes downright false, even with the best of intentions; but it is part of the picture. The key is to remember that, as historians, we make

---

[18]Hannah Arendt, *Eichmann on Jerusalem: A Report in the Banality of Evil* (New York: Penguin, 1963); HD advocates claim that Höss's confession and memoirs are discredited by the fact that he was initially mistreated by the British soldiers who captured him. While he was indeed severely beaten by his captors on arrest, there is no evidence of subsequent ill-treatment during his trial or while he awaited death, the time during which he wrote his memoirs.

no claims for our statements beyond that which the evidence will bear. And eyewitness testimony and personal testimony, if left in isolation, will sustain only very provisional and highly qualified statements at best.

This is where we need to reflect on other forms of evidence. With the Holocaust, thankfully, there is much with which we can work. Take, for example, archaeological evidence: there are camps, there are gas chambers, or ruins thereof, there are traces of Zyklon-B in the walls. Again, we have seen from the work of Leuchter that such evidence can perhaps not stand simply on its own, but the case for the Holocaust does not simply depend upon these artifacts. There are photographs and films, some taken by the Nazis themselves, some taken by inmates such as the Sonderkommandos, and some taken by the armies of liberation. Well, you might claim, photos can be doctored and changed to be very misleading, and, even if individual photographs are genuine, a picture of a pile of dead bodies or a group of Nazis shooting a group of Jews does not necessarily prove that the Holocaust happened. But, remember, what is emerging is a matrix of evidence, no single element of which, taken in isolation, is decisive but which, when taken as a whole, starts to possess a cumulative, convicting power. In matters of historical evidence, the sum of the whole is always greater than the sum of the parts, and the mere poking of holes in fragments of the parts, such as the disproving of a detail of an eyewitness account, is not enough by itself to undermine the power of the cumulative general case.

Then, beyond the evidence of the memoirs and confessions, the camps themselves, and the photographic record, there are the corroborative elements from the Nazi world: the mountains of anti-Semitic propaganda, the occurrence of *Kristallnacht* in 1938, when Jewish businesses were ransacked, and, of course, contemporary documentary evidence from the Nazi leaders that something terrible was being planned and performed on the Jewish population. There are the minutes of the Wannsee Conference of 1941, taken by Eichmann and corrected by Reinhard Heydrich, Himmler's second-in-command, in which the systematic liquidation of Jews is discussed. Interestingly enough, the minutes used euphemisms throughout for what was being planned; but this was exposed by Eichmann himself in his 1961 testimony at his own trial. Then there is the report from Gerhard

Riegner, director of the Geneva Office of the World Jewish Congress from 1939 to 1945, to the British Foreign Office, dated August 8, 1942, that he had received word from a well-connected German source that the Nazis were planning to gas between three and four million Jews.[19] We might also mention the comments made by Foreign Minister von Ribbentrop, in Hitler's presence, in answer to a question from the Hungarian leader, Miklós Horthy, as to what he should do about the Jews: annihilate them or take them to concentration camps.[20] Taken in isolation, none of these strands of evidence is perhaps powerful enough to provide a knock-out punch, but taken together the case surely becomes irresistible.

As one final point, it is worth noting that the twisting of evidence by HD advocates is not restricted to Leuchter-style readings of the bricks and mortar of Auschwitz; it also extends to written documents as well. Of course, the pop cliché about postmodernism is that texts have no fixed meaning. There is a certain truth in this in the sense that texts are the result of complex actions and can never be understood exhaustively; but does this mean that their meaning is simply plastic and can be made into anything that the reader, or reading community, wishes? Or that everything can be reduced to the model of a "text," a move which is itself highly contentious? Is genocide suitably described as a "text," I wonder?

To take a specific example, it is worth looking at one such "text," a phone log from Heinrich Himmler's office, to see how it has been used in the debates about the Holocaust.[21] The log refers to a phone conversation between Himmler and Heydrich, then in Prague, on November 30, 1941. The log summary reads as follows:

Verhaftung Dr Jekelius.
Angebl. Sohn Molotow.
Judentrasnport aus Berlin.
Keine Liquidierung.

---

[19]Cited by Evans in *Lying about Hitler*, 129.
[20]Ibid., 93.
[21]In the following paragraphs, I am dependent upon the discussion of this text in Evans, *Lying about Hitler*, 79ff.

This is very straightforward German and translates as "Arrest of Dr Jekelius. Supposed son of Molotov. Jew-transport from Berlin. No Liquidation." Now, in the introduction to the first edition of his book, *Hitler's War*, Irving referred to this as "incontrovertible evidence" that "Hitler ordered on November 30, 1941, that there was to be 'no liquidation' of the Jews" and even referred to the fact that he, Irving, had seen the handwritten note on this.

But is this what the note says? Nothing in the note would imply that this was a general order, coming from the very top of the Reich, concerning the broad policy relative to Jews. Thus, to make the general claim that Irving does requires the establishment of a broader context for the note that would imply this meaning. Thus, the first thing Richard Evans did relative to this document in his research for Deborah Lipstadt's defense team, was to search the SS records relative to the East to see if there had been a particular transportation of Jews from Berlin immediately prior to this date. In fact, as he discovered, there had been: on November 27 of that year, a trainload of Jews had been transported from Berlin and had arrived in Riga on November 29–30. This was immediately prior to a massacre of the local Jewish population by the SS chief in the area, Friedrich Jeckeln, who then added the Berlin Jews to his tally by having them machine gunned to death along with the rest. Thus, a little bit of digging into the background of the phone call would strongly imply that this was a specific order relating to one trainload of Jews.

Further, for Irving's reading of the text to hold water, one might have expected other events to have taken place in the immediately previous context. If the phrase "no liquidation" was an order from Hitler himself, one might have anticipated that there would be some records of Himmler either visiting Hitler or receiving a phone call or communication from him in the days before this phone conversation. In addition, the log itself does not even make it clear whether it was Himmler who called Heydrich or the other way around.

In other words, digging into the immediate historical context of the phone log strongly implies that the straightforward reading of the text as indicating specific orders about a specific transportation of Jews from

Berlin is indeed the correct one. To argue as Irving did that this is evidence of an order from the very top of the Reich structure to forbid liquidation of Jews in general is to place an interpretation on the log entry that not only speculates well beyond the wording of the text itself but also flies in the face of the corroborative evidence that effectively verifies the natural reading of the words.

All of this points to the importance of context in the analysis of individual historical artifacts. Whether dealing with a handwritten note, a potsherd, the remains of a building, or a photograph, there is a sense in which the postmoderns are right in saying that texts have no fixed meaning: in isolation, each of these pieces of evidence is somewhat less than fully adequate in helping us to construct a historical narrative; none of them, if you like, is its own interpretation. But as the historian starts to connect one historical artifact to another, an account of the past becomes possible, and, dare I say it, some accounts start to look more true than others.

It is this aspect of history, corroboration and verification, that allows us to dismiss HD as nonsense while yet take seriously the debates between intentionalists and functionalists, respecting the latter two groups as proper contributors to historical knowledge. These scholars do not deny the existence of gas chambers at Auschwitz or the fact that the Third Reich pursued genocide on a grand technological scale that was unprecedented and driven primarily by racial hatred. They accept that the historical artifacts and evidence indicate clearly that a large number of Jews were liquidated by the Nazis. On that there is no dispute. What they differ over is how these non-negotiable facts should be interpreted relative to overall Nazi policy: to repeat, did this intentional genocide emerge over a period of time or was it an integral part of the Nazi agenda from the very beginning?

Can Historians Change Their Minds?

Some may respond at this point and say, "Hang on a minute! All historians are biased, and thus how can this kind of corroboration and analysis be done in a neutral way that gets us to the truth?" To this I would answer: it cannot be done neutrally; the historian's own perspective will always shape how he selects and reads the evidence. But it is a huge leap to go from there to saying that all histories are equally valid, or that history is ultimately all about aesthetics. Historians can find evidence that overturns even some of their deepest held convictions and change their views accordingly. Indeed, one of my favorite church history anecdotes is about just such an occurrence.

On October 28, 1518, Oswald Myconius wrote his friend, Huldrych Zwingli, then parish priest in Einsiedeln, informing him that there was a pastoral vacancy at the Great Minster in Zurich and urging him to apply for the position. He followed this letter, however, with a second on December 3, indicating that various objections had been raised to Zwingli's candidacy, including one that he was unable to address: that he had fornicated with the daughter of a prominent citizen in Einsiedeln. Such a failing was not uncommon among priests in the sixteenth century, any more than one suspects it is today. Indeed, one of the other priestly candidates was supposed to have fathered six children. What made it significant, of course, was Zwingli's future role as a Reformer and thus as one who proactively helped to dismantle the notion of clerical celibacy as the norm. Zwingli's sexual incontinence would become a propaganda coup for the Catholics. Now, there was never any known corroborative evidence for this, and many assumed that the rumor was a piece of malice put about by Zwingli's enemies and kept alive by Catholic propagandists who wished to portray the Reformation as driven not so much by theology as by the desire of the Reformers to escape from the strictures of priestly celibacy and indulge in sexual license.

From a historian's perspective, this is a classic problem: a claim made by an unknown and unverifiable source, and then debated in sources that are either openly hostile to or uncritically allied with the accused. It is similar to the problem that early church historians face in reconstructing the views of heretical movements: given that the orthodox were assiduous in destroying the writings of their vanquished foes, often the only access we get to the writings of early church heretics is through quotations embedded in texts written by their enemies, or in summaries of their thought provided by the same. In either case, the witness is hostile and, taken in isolation, the views expressed in the source are rightly subject to suspicion.

Returning to Zwingli and his alleged failing, there was, as mentioned, no corroborative evidence by which the claim could be verified; but then, in the nineteenth century, something happened in the archives in Zurich. Distinguished Zwingli scholar, Johannes Schulthess, discovered there a letter from Zwingli, replying to the charge of fornication, in which he admitted that he had indeed committed the sin of unchastity, despite his great efforts to the contrary, but also stated that this chapter of his life was now closed and he was living a holy and chaste life. At the time, Schulthess was with his student, Alexander Schweizer, who was himself to become a great historical dogmatician, and he showed the letter to the young man before he placed it into the flame of the candle on the desk. The meaning of the move was obvious: Schulthess had discovered evidence that tarnished the reputation of his hero, and, as a Zwingli scholar, his task was to polish the edifice, to maintain the great man's reputation, not sully it with the sleaze of everyday life. Then, after a moment's thought, he removed the document from the flame and extinguished the fire, so as to preserve what was left. Turning to Schweizer he said (in a moment of true methodological greatness), "Protestantism is the truth in all circumstances."[22]

The story is interesting and instructive, not simply because of its rather dramatic elements (OK, not dramatic by Shakespearean standards, but this is the practice of church history we are discussing!) but also because it shows that, confronted with a text that simply could not be assimilated to the Zwingli-as-godly-hero paradigm to which Schulthess was committed, Schulthess neither twisted the text (short of claiming it was a forgery, it is hard to see how he could have done such a thing) nor destroyed it (which he was very clearly tempted to do). No, he changed his mind. He

---

[22]The story is told in W. P. Stephens, *Zwingli: An Introduction to His Thought* (Oxford: Clarendon Press, 1992), 17.

took account of the evidence and reworked his understanding of Zwingli as a result. Does this mean he understood the letter exhaustively? No. Presumably, he did not know exactly what thoughts were flowing through Zwingli's mind when he wrote it, or all the nuances of the impact Zwingli intended by it; but Schulthess knew that, whatever else it meant, it certainly indicated that the idea that Zwingli had been framed by opponents and falsely accused could no longer be maintained.

Most, if not all, competent historians will be able to tell similar anecdotes, even if they lack the dramatic power of this particular example. I well remember as a postgraduate student, studying the theology of select English Reformers in the reigns of Henry VIII, Edward VI, and Mary, how much I wanted William Tyndale to be a good, solid Lutheran on the issue of justification by faith. After all, he translated and utilized Luther's texts extensively in his own writings. Nevertheless, the more I studied Tyndale's use of Luther's works, the more I came to realize that fundamental aspects of Luther's thought were missing from Tyndale, that he used the German Reformer as a source but transformed his ideas as he embedded them in his own writings. Notions such as imputation and the theology of the cross, so crucial to Luther, were simply absent or profoundly muted in Tyndale. Tyndale spoke much more about the work of the Holy Spirit and about the positive role of the Law than Luther would ever have countenanced; and his covenant theology played into his view of the sacraments in a way that really placed him closer to Zwingli, Luther's hated opponent on the matter of the Lord's Supper. Reluctantly, the texts drove me to revise my initial working thesis—that Tyndale was simply an English Lutheran— and to see him as far more eclectic, and far closer to the Zurich theology than I had originally imagined.

Later I studied the writings of John Hooper, famous for his opposition to clerical vestments under Edward VI. Again, my preconceived notion was that this made him an early Puritan, and I fully expected to find a commitment to predestinarian theology, especially since he had studied in Zurich and was friends with Heinrich Bullinger. In fact, close reading of his texts indicated that, on predestination, he borrowed heavily from Luther's lieutenant, Philip Melanchthon, and held to a position on the matter fairly close to the semi-Pelagianism of Erasmus. That he engaged in ferocious and personal debate with a Calvinist, Bartholomew Traheron, on the issue, confirmed that Hooper was no predestinarian in either the Genevan or Zurich sense of the word. I was forced to revise my analysis accordingly.

Of course, to the theoreticians of postmodernism, committed to the infinitely malleable nature of texts, such occurrences are hard to explain; but such theoreticians are rarely practitioners of history, and such of them as profess to be historians are rarely consistent in their historical writing with their philosophical claims made elsewhere. There is a difference, in other words, between what they say and what they do. Most historians, by contrast, while perhaps not being able to articulate the philosophical rationale behind the possibility of such changes, yet find this their everyday experience: they have a working hypothesis; they test it by evidence; and they reject it, modify it, or affirm it on the basis of the evidence. It is not, as the saying goes, rocket science.

Conclusion

In concluding this chapter, let me recap the basic points I have tried to make. First, it seems to be obvious (though it is paraded as some sort of profound, brilliant insight by too many these days) that no historian writes neutral history and thus that every historical narrative reflects the author's own approach in some measure, both as to selection of evidence, shaping of story, and various emphases and purposes. This does not, however, require me to accept that all histories are equally valid or engage in the kind of naïve posturing that equates "unbiased" with "objective." Objectivity is not neutrality: as a Marxist historian writes Marxist history that can be read, appreciated, appropriated, and critiqued by a non-Marxist, so this is possible because both Marxists and non-Marxists build their case on publicly accessible and publicly assessable evidence. Even a writer like David Novick, who writes a history of history in order to prove that objectivity is an impossible dream, does so in a way that, despite his claims to the contrary, conforms to established canons of historical writing and is arguably objective. Objectivity is much more modest, and thus a much more attainable category than neutrality.

The phenomenon of Holocaust Denial offers a great opportunity for exploring this idea, for if the referentiality of history is dismissed as irrelevant or impossible to establish, then there can really be no response to HD other than on the moral or aesthetic grounds that its conclusions are evil or distasteful. In fact, exploration of aspects of HD brings into clear focus what is and is not good historical method, and the important distinction Richard Evans makes between method and theory is important here. In actual fact, there is a remarkable consensus among practicing historians over what constitutes good method: verification, correlation of evidence, awareness of the strengths and limitations of different types of evidence, etc. Historians may, and do frequently, disagree over the significance of historical actions and events, but there is usually general agreement over the actual reality of such events. The Battle of Waterloo did happen, as did the Holocaust; but Elvis did not fake his death in 1977 in order to take up a job as a shelf stacker in Grand Haven, Michigan.

This is not to deny that historical method does not come without philosophical commitments. Of course it does. The external reality of the world; the independence of events from my own self-consciousness; the notion that there is such a thing as time and that certain events and actions take place before others—all of these represent philosophical commitments. But for most if not all historians, these are not contentious issues. Far from being issues over which historians do battle, they are generally assumed, as are the basic rules of verification that all historians routinely employ whereby one piece of evidence is connected to another and so on, and as the context is elaborated and one piece of evidence is corroborated by another, a more detailed picture of the past emerges. This picture is not an exhaustive one, for sure, and is certainly not without the fingerprints of the historian on it; but it is certainly one that can be challenged, modified, and improved by criteria on which all historians are in basic agreement. That is why I know that Holocaust Denial is nonsense: because I can prove the Holocaust happened and my history of it, while far from perfect, yet does justice to the historical evidence in a way that HD does not.

This points us to the next question, that of theory, and to the issue of explanatory schemes and frameworks in history. Thus, in the next chapter we turn to look at this equally contentious topic.

CHAPTER 2

Grand Schemes and Misdemeanors

History is not the same as the past. It is rather a re-presentation of the past, or, in the phrase of John Lukacs, it is "remembered past," with all of the contingency and limitations that such implies. Indeed, Lukacs's phrase is useful because it also brings into play the role of the historian: the historian is doing the "remembering," not, of course, necessarily or even typically as an eyewitness, but as one who is involved in the production of history as an agent, one who brings to bear categories, priorities, etc., in order to construct a coherent narrative. Historical actions and events are ineradicably complex; no single historian can ever hope to capture all of the complexity. Thus, history is necessarily selective, and this selectivity is shaped by the historian.

To state the obvious in a rather blunt way, when you read a book about the Battle of Waterloo, you are not taking part in said battle; you are looking at ink marks on a page. The book is the action of an author at a later date, and the pathway from the battle to the book is undoubtedly a complex one, involving the historian selecting evidence, ordering said evidence into a coherent narrative, and offering some kind of explanation of what was going on at the battle. If the historian is interested in military strategy and battlefield tactics, then the book will no doubt focus on the specific actions of various groups on the actual battlefield. If the historian is interested in European diplomacy of the early nineteenth century, then the focus may be less on ground-level troop maneuvers and more on the role the battle as a whole played within the larger European scene. And if the historian is interested in the lives of Napoleon or Wellington, then attention will be paid to the battle in the context of their respective careers.

In each case, historians operate with certain rules or principles for selecting, arranging, and interpreting the material. In other words, they apply certain categories that help to bring retrospective order out of the past; these categories are part of the explanatory schemes that make history possible as a discipline, and every historian operates with such schemes, whether or not they are aware of them or care to acknowledge them. Of course, the burden of this book is simply to make historians more self-conscious about their role in the writing of history, and thus it is important that we spend some time reflecting on the potential hazards and pitfalls that are involved when it comes to explanatory schemes.

If we were to look back over the history of history itself, we would see that the discipline (if we can use the singular) cannot be represented by any single explanatory scheme, but has exhibited dramatic variations in both content and complexity over the years. To look at the Homeric epics of the *Odyssey* and the *Iliad* is to look at texts which tell of a time that is located at some indeterminate point in the past; and in these accounts, things happen variously because of individual human emotions or passions and because of erratic interventions by the gods. Only by very close reading of the text are we able to discern anything about the wider world of these texts, and then we are more likely learning about the wider world of the author(s) than of the participants in the actual Trojan War. Homer's explanatory scheme, if we can call it such, is, of course, a far cry from later approaches, whether that of medieval Joachim of Fiore, or later writers such as Vico, Hegel, Marx, or Fukuyama. But all historians operate with certain notions of what it is that drives human action and provides the dynamic for history, and each of these writers was committed to a view of the world that profoundly shaped the way they explained the events they saw taking place around them and in the past.

The strengths of explanatory schemes are obvious: they allow for a coherent narrative account of the past, which does more than simply list events on a piece of paper as if they were isolated, unconnected happenings; rather they offer ways of establishing causal or influential points of connection between such events in a way that brings out the reasons why specific things happened in the way they did. This is why good historians do not write in bullet points, something which seems increasingly difficult to communicate to students reared on PowerPoint and texting as the chosen media for communication. Historians do not think in isolated sound bites; they think in terms of larger patterns and networks of happenings. To give a very simple example: the statements "Germany invaded Poland on September 1, 1939; Britain declared war on Germany, September 3, 1939" are both true but require some connection in order to be meaningful. "Germany invaded Poland on September 1, 1939, and Britain declared war two days later because of her treaty obligations to guarantee the safety of Poland from German aggression" is something that connects the two statements in a purposeful, explanatory way. The historian provides a connective rationale that indicates the relationship between the two events.

That is a very simple, almost bullet-point like example. A more elaborate example might, perhaps, be the rise to power of Adolf Hitler in the first place. To explain why the most technologically, philosophically, economically, and culturally advanced nation in Europe came under the sway of an ideology as (at least from our vantage point today) self-evidently crazy as that of the Nazis is a fascinating and complicated undertaking; and, in order even to begin approaching an answer to the subject, various issues need to be taken into account. First, there is the humiliation of Germany's defeat in the First World War, which helped set the scene for national resentment and, indeed, for refueling nationalism. Second, there were the demobbed soldiers, hardened by battle and the violence of war, returning home in defeat and looking for a public voice and an outlet for their frustration. Then there was the crushing economic burden of reparations, imposed by the victors in the Versailles Treaty, again something which provided fuel for resentment and nationalism. There was also the economic depression of the early 1930s, which put pressure on democratic institutions as they appeared inadequate to cope with the situation. On a broader canvas, there were the legacies of nineteenth-century German nationalism and, to a lesser degree, anti-Semitism. And one could also mention the fear of the lower middle class that they were being dramatically squeezed between the rich and the poor, and seeing their own status in society being significantly downgraded. Each of these factors (and surely many more) played a role and must be taken into account by any historian who wants to explain the Nazi Party's electoral success and later consolidation of power.

A moment's reflection on these factors also reveals something else: my inclusion of each of these indicates that I have an underlying view of how the world operates which makes me consider these significant points to help explain the rise of Nazism. I am aware, for example, that economics has a profound impact on behavior. Money talks, and money motivates as well. A starving man without a home will do things that someone with a full belly and nice house in the suburbs would never contemplate. I am also aware that cultural background has an impact: somebody repeatedly told from birth that Jews are inferior and whose only knowledge of Jews is refracted through anti-Semitic propaganda will inevitably look upon Jews differently from someone who grew up with many Jewish friends.

There is nothing profound about any of this; but it is clear from such that, whether I have reflected on the matter in any depth, I do have some form of explanatory scheme with which I am working. This scheme may be eclectic, and it may be little more than an understanding of how certain things influence certain other things, but nonetheless this does provide me with general principles for connecting historical actions and phenomena that I might otherwise not connect.

It is also evident that this will shape the kind of evidence that I gather. For example, if I believe that economics is significant, I will look at economic data such as rates of inflation and unemployment. If I believe propaganda is important, I will look at the films, newscasts, pamphlets, and speeches being made. If I believe the Versailles Treaty is important, I will look at how it was represented in German culture, what economic impact it had, and how it functioned in internal political debates and also in foreign policy.

It is worth noting, however, that my explanatory scheme can be held fairly loosely; and, indeed, I would argue that it should be so. In believing that, say, the rate of inflation is important, I am not committed to believing that it is important in a particular way or in the same way everywhere and at all times. This is where the historian's task is not simply that of bringing a hard-and-fast model to bear and merely gathering data that confirms it; good historians operate with hypothetical explanatory schemes that are subject to correction by the evidence gathered. This is important, as it reflects that important principle articulated so well by Richard Evans: there is a distinction between theory and method. And, contrary to so much pop postmodernism, the relationship is not one whereby theory simply determines method and is thus incorrigible; rather, theory should be held loosely, as a hypothesis, and subject always to correction in light of the standard procedures of the historical profession: corroboration, verification, and falsification. Historical explanatory schemes should be heuristic not prescriptive.

However, it is the case that history has often been pursued by those committed to a very tight and closed view of what the world is and how it operates; and in these contexts, explanatory schemes operate as much as expositions of particular philosophies as they do heuristic frameworks that allow some kind of interpretation of the past. There are numerous examples one could cite in this context but perhaps the most influential is that of Marxism. Marxism, possibly more than any other explanatory scheme, has done sterling service in drawing attention to the importance of economics and of material factors in understanding historical actions; but in its attempt to explain the fundamental dynamic of historical movement in terms of class struggle, it overreaches itself. Nevertheless, given the fact that, in reaction to Marxism, many, at least at a popular level, shy away from reflecting on economic factors as important in history, especially in texts that do not seem to speak to such matters directly, it is worth prefacing our discussion of Marxism by spending a few moments reflecting on how economic factors can and should shape the way we understand the past.

The Importance of Economics

Economic factors are often neglected by historians in my own discipline of intellectual history. As this area tends to be preoccupied with ideas, and ideas seem, in origin at least, to be abstract and immaterial, and to exist primarily in that strange ethereal world between our ears, to take into account economics would seem at first glance to involve a confusion of categories. Economics is rather material; my ideas are rather immaterial. Yet a moment's reflection will quickly reveal to us that how we think and behave are profoundly shaped by economic factors. If my house is already overcrowded and I cannot afford a larger one, it will no doubt have an impact on how many more children I believe I should have; if I have access to contraception, it will no doubt shape my understanding of the function of sex; and if the area in which I live does not have enough jobs even for the local residents, it might well shape how I view outsiders moving in to my neighborhood. The historian, even the historian of ideas, cannot afford to ignore material questions when addressing how and why events and actions in the past occurred in the manner in which they did.

In order to explore this, let us look at a good example of a text that is susceptible to asking questions from an economic perspective, and which then yields an explanation that might otherwise have been missed. This is also a text which, when examined from this economic perspective, reveals more than the author perhaps intends, and further provides opportunity to the budding historian for seeing the complexity of human action and the importance of careful contextualization, of close reading, and of asking questions. This text is the famous letter of Pliny the Younger to the Emperor Trajan regarding a recent outbreak of Christianity in the area where Pliny was governor, Pontus/Bithynia (modern northern Turkey). I reproduce the letter in full:

> It is my practice, my lord, to refer to you all matters concerning which I am in doubt. For who can better give guidance to my hesitation or inform my ignorance? I have never participated in trials of Christians. I therefore do not know what offenses it is the practice to punish or investigate, and to what extent. And I have been not a little hesitant as to whether there should be

any distinction on account of age or no difference between the very young and the more mature; whether pardon is to be granted for repentance, or, if a man has once been a Christian, it does him no good to have ceased to be one; whether the name itself, even without offenses, or only the offenses associated with the name are to be punished.

Meanwhile, in the case of those who were denounced to me as Christians, I have observed the following procedure: I interrogated these as to whether they were Christians; those who confessed I interrogated a second and a third time, threatening them with punishment; those who persisted I ordered executed. For I had no doubt that, whatever the nature of their creed, stubbornness and inflexible obstinacy surely deserve to be punished. There were others possessed of the same folly; but because they were Roman citizens, I signed an order for them to be transferred to Rome.

Soon accusations spread, as usually happens, because of the proceedings going on, and several incidents occurred. An anonymous document was published containing the names of many persons. Those who denied that they were or had been Christians, when they invoked the gods in words dictated by me, offered prayer with incense and wine to your image, which I had ordered to be brought for this purpose together with statues of the gods, and moreover cursed Christ—none of which those who are really Christians, it is said, can be forced to do—these I thought should be discharged. Others named by the informer declared that they were Christians, but then denied it, asserting that they had been but had ceased to be, some three years before, others many years, some as much as twenty-five years. They all worshipped your image and the statues of the gods, and cursed Christ.

They asserted, however, that the sum and substance of their fault or error had been that they were accustomed to meet on a fixed day before dawn and sing responsively a hymn to Christ as to a god, and to bind themselves by oath, not to some crime, but not to commit fraud, theft, or adultery, not falsify their trust, nor to refuse to return a trust when called upon to do so. When this was over, it was their custom to depart and to assemble again to partake of food—but ordinary and innocent food. Even this, they affirmed, they had ceased to do after my edict by which, in accordance with your instructions, I had forbidden political associations. Accordingly, I judged it all the more necessary to find out what the truth was by torturing two female slaves who were called deaconesses. But I discovered nothing else but depraved, excessive superstition.

I therefore postponed the investigation and hastened to consult you. For the matter seemed to me to warrant consulting you, especially because of the number involved. For many persons of every age, every rank, and also of both sexes are and will be endangered. For the contagion of this super-stition has spread not only to the cities but also to the villages and farms. But it seems possible to check and cure it. It is certainly quite clear that the temples, which had been almost deserted, have begun to be frequented, that the established religious rites, long neglected, are being resumed, and that from everywhere sacrificial animals are coming, for which until now very few purchasers could be found. Hence it is easy to imagine what a multitude of people can be reformed if an opportunity for repentance is afforded.[1]

There are a number of comments we could make about this text. The most obvious and superficial is what it tells us about Christianity in Pontus/ Bithynia at the start of the second century. According to Pliny, Christianity was alive and well in this area at this point.

Now, Pliny gives us a firsthand, eyewitness account, so first we should ask ourselves whether we have reason to doubt the reliability of what he recounts. He does not seem panicked; and it is unlikely that he is recounting an event that happened years ago, which has since become overlaid with years of retelling, or of listening to and absorbing, the accounts of others. Crucially, we also have no reason to doubt that Pliny is simply describing what has been told to him by the individuals he has interrogated because his account scarcely strengthens his reasons for punishing the Christians. If anything, we would expect him to be inclined to sensationalize what he is describing by playing up any juicy or extreme aspects of their behavior to which he is privy, but he presents the information (from his perspec-tive, rather bland and nondescript) in a remarkably matter-of-fact manner. Thus, he tells us that the Christians meet to sing hymns; they worship Christ as a God; they eat food, but only ordinary food, as Pliny indicates; and they pledge themselves to live moral lives. None of this is incredible;

---

[1]Pliny the Younger, Letters 10.96–97, Internet Medieval Sourcebook, http://www.fordham.edu/ halsall/source/pliny1.html/.

and, given my warnings about the need for verification and/or corroboration as strengthening our confidence in eyewitness testimony, all of it tallies with what we can establish from other historical sources. The use of hymns, the divinity of Christ, and the eating of food are all attested to in the New Testament documents, of which Pliny was almost certainly ignorant. Thus, the fact that what he says is consistent with these is good grounds for believing that this is a pretty straightforward description of what went on. Further, that Pliny goes out of his way to emphasize the *ordinary* nature of the food which they eat seems to point clearly to the fact that he was probably aware of the contemporary allegations that Christians were cannibals, something against which the Greek Apologists were constantly defending themselves and whose testimony thus serves as corroboration once again of the basic reliability of Pliny's statement. On this level, the letter of Pliny is another pebble on the pile of evidence about early Christian practices.

But there is so much more than just this surface reading of the text yields. Now, there are some questions that the text cannot be asked because it simply cannot answer. Was Ann Boleyn a witch? Why did Napoleon lose at Waterloo? Is Elvis really dead? Would these Christians have liked eating curry? All are inappropriate because this text does not address these issues directly, nor does it contain implicit information that might be of help. The text itself delimits the questions that can be asked. Yet setting the letter in a broader context and engaging in a careful examination of its internal content does allow us to infer a lot more than the fact that, on the surface, it offers us no more than reliable insight into early Christian worship and Roman imperial process.

First, we know from other letters of Pliny that he was an imperial sycophant, always eager to please his master back in Rome. Once we connect this to the content of this letter, we have reason to question Pliny's claim that he is unaware of the appropriate process relative to investigating and punishing Christians. If he were as ignorant of appropriate procedure and precedent as he claims to be, he would scarcely have executed these Christians, let alone executed them for arrogance, for to have done so would have risked the wrath of the emperor, not something a man like Pliny would have casually courted. That Pliny had enjoyed preferment as an imperial functionary under the brutal emperor, Domitian, a man whose passion for the cult of emperor worship had brought him into collision with the Jews (and, presumably, Christians) would make it likely that he was well aware of the scope of his powers in this regard. Thus, it seems more likely that Pliny has acted as he has done in order to ingratiate himself with Trajan; the pleas of ignorance are probably a device designed to provoke a "well done, thou good and faithful servant" reaction. We can infer this, as noted above, by setting the text in the context of other information we have about Pliny's life; knowledge of the individual agent is always important in interpreting his or her individual actions.

Second, and perhaps the most interesting question that I want to ask of the text is this: why were these Christians persecuted here? Now, the reaction of many Christians today to this question might be a straightforward claim that the Bible says that Christians will be persecuted because they are light in a dark and hostile world. Others might say that Christians, with their claims to having a monopoly on the truth, would have seemed arrogant in a pluralist society such as Rome, where such religious exclusivism made them difficult to assimilate and, during periods of the enforcement of emperor worship, impossible so to do. Both claims could be true; but then the problem is why Christians were not persecuted consistently throughout the Roman Empire, given that these explanations are based on universal characteristics and not specific to this situation. So, I pose my question once again: why were these Christians persecuted in this particular place at this particular time?

The answer to why these Christians were being persecuted here is surely in large part tied up with the question of who it is who is informing on them. Pliny tells the emperor that numerous anonymous accusations were made against this group. If we can find out who made them, we might have a better idea of why the persecution broke out. At first glance, the text does not appear to help us identify who they were; but a closer reading gives a very significant clue as to who these informers might have been. The key to solving the problem is in the following passage:

It is certainly quite clear that the temples, which had been almost deserted, have begun to be frequented, that the established religious rites, long neglected, are being resumed, and that from everywhere sacrificial animals are coming, for which until now very few purchasers could be found.

What Pliny tells us here, almost as an aside, is that the local economy, connected to the temple cult, its religious rites, and the related trade in sacrificial animals, has improved since he dealt with the Christians. This, in turn, allows us to infer that, quite probably, the presence of Christians has put significant economic pressure on certain sections of the community, particularly those whose livelihoods depended upon the temple trade, a trade that, of course, suffered as the temple cult declined in the face of this new competition. So why were the Christians persecuted here at this point in time? One plausible hypothesis is that it was the economic hardship they caused, and, given this, it is therefore also plausible to surmise that the anonymous accusations might well have arisen from the section of the population that suffered most.

Pliny tells us, perhaps unintentionally, that the local economy has suffered; and this offers us a reason why persecution happens here, and not necessarily elsewhere, at this particular moment in time. Some might want to argue that this is a somewhat speculative theory, but there are a number of responses to that. First, as has been the burden of this book to demonstrate, while no historical explanation can claim to offer a single, exhaustive explanation as to why anything happens, some explanations make better sense, given the evidence and our status of knowledge, and some are plain wrong. In this case, I would suggest that my interpretation— that the persecution is connected to the economic downturn in the local temple economy—is plausible, in that it is consistent with what Pliny tells us. Others may disagree with me, but in doing so, they should offer a more plausible account of the matter than the one I have presented.

Second, I would support my thesis by pointing to other documents that indicate a connection between economic hardship and persecution of this kind. For example, Mark's Gospel, chapter 5 contains an account of a man possessed by demons. Jesus heals this man, and then is asked to leave by a scared population. One might have thought that cleaning up the neighborhood by returning to his right mind a man who was clearly a public menace would in itself have endeared Jesus to the local population. So why were they scared, and why did they immediately move to encourage him to leave the area? Well, the text tells us that the exorcism of the man involved the death of "a great herd of pigs" (Mark 5:11). Presumably, then, the fear and loathing that the local people showed for Jesus—surprising given how he had presumably just solved a major local problem!—is surely connected to the catastrophic impact his actions must have had on the local economy, built as it presumably was on supplying pork to the occupying forces in the Decapolis, an area where we know there was a large Gentile population.

Again, an economic connection can also be found for a famous event in Acts, where Luke describes the riot that takes place after Paul preaches at Ephesus. A superficial, or perhaps a pious, reading of the passage would seem to indicate that the riot was triggered by the affront that Paul's preaching was to the goddess Artemis. Yet a closer look reveals something else. Here is how Luke records the event:

> About that time, there arose no little disturbance concerning the Way. For a man named Demetrius, a silversmith, who made silver shrines of Artemis, brought no little business to the craftsmen. These he gathered together, with the workmen in similar trades, and said, "Men, you know that from this business we have our wealth. And you see and hear that not only in Ephesus but in almost all of Asia this Paul has persuaded and turned away a great many people, saying that gods made with hands are not gods. And there is danger not only that this trade of ours may come into disrepute but also that the temple of the great goddess Artemis may be counted as nothing, and that she may even be deposed from her magnificence, she whom all Asia and the world worship."
>
> When they heard this they were enraged and were crying out, "Great is Artemis of the Ephesians!" (Acts 19:23–28)

Now, one does not want to be cynical and underestimate the piety of these Artemis worshipers in Ephesus, but the way Luke records the event makes it clear that he wants the reader to see a definite economic connection between the damage that Paul's preaching has done to the local trade for the silversmith and his colleagues and the riot that subsequently occurs. Offended pagan piety provides the idiom by which Demetrius expresses his real concerns with Paul's teaching: it is doing damage to his income and his standard of living.

In each of these three instances, the texts—of Pliny, of Mark, and of Luke—offer insights into the economic background to religious persecution. In pointing this out, I am not trying to reduce religious persecution to a simple question of economics. Indeed, that would be simplistic. Just as ideological or theological commitment is, by itself, frequently an insufficient reason for a particular persecution to occur at a particular place at a particular time, so economics by itself cannot offer an exhaustive account of why things happen. The broader context of the persecution of Jews in medieval Europe, for example, included the noneconomic fact that they were simply unassimilable to a society built upon a close identification of the state and the Christian church, and so their position was always precarious. Further, even in the last example above, that of the riot in Ephesus, it seems unlikely that all of those rioting were driven by fear, conscious or unconscious, of the imminent collapse of the silversmith's business. Hedonism—the sheer fun to be had by rioting and smashing things up—no doubt played its part, as did the desire not to see the traditional piety and religion of the city subverted. My purpose here is not to offer economic explanations as alternatives to others, but to argue that the texts show that economic factors were significant, and that any historical explanation must do justice to that and draw out the complexity of historical events by acknowledging the complexity of human agency.

Finally, and as a necessary caveat, I would also stress that my interpretation of the evidence remains a plausible explanation, not a hard-and-fast claim to absolute and exhaustive truth. It has the status of a hypothesis that accounts effectively for the current state of the evidence. It is possible that my theory could be directly verified by the discovery of a cache of letters in which the local temple merchants write to each other to cook up a plan to inform on the Christians to Pliny on the grounds that, unless they do so, they will go out of business. Or, a cache of letters could turn up in which it is clear that the anonymous informants were not the temple merchants at all but militant members of the local temple cult, angry that Christianity was detracting from the honor of the local gods. Such evidence would falsify my thesis, or at least require substantial modification of it.

Such connections between economic factors and individual action are interesting. But for some historians, economics became not only the dominant key to understanding history, it became virtually the only key to understanding history. Such were the Marxists. And Marxism does not just provide a great example of how economics can be used by historians, but it also allows us to reflect on the shortcomings of grand explanatory schemes.

Marxism

Alongside that of Freud, and possibly Nietzsche, the thought of Karl Marx was undoubtedly one of the single most significant intellectual forces in the twentieth century, not simply transforming the way academics operated in the classroom, but inspiring revolutions, transforming the political map of the world, costing millions of individuals across the globe their lives, and millions more their freedom. Yet, when he died in 1883, only a handful of people attended his funeral; and any who were walking through Highgate Cemetery that day and heard his longtime friend, collaborator, and patron, Friedrich Engels, making a bombastic speech about how the whole world would one day know Marx's name, would have thought he was just another bearded nutter of the kind with which nineteenth-century London was no doubt all too familiar. Yet, nutter or not, Engels was prophetic, and within fifty years Marxism had not only inspired a revolution in Russia, it was also making remarkable headway into the thought of many intellectuals. Indeed, to young people in Europe in the 1930s, Marxism seemed like the only viable option for presenting a coherent alternative to fascism and Nazism, also on the rise across the continent. That is perhaps the most charitable explanation for why so many thoughtful intellectuals, from George Bernard Shaw to W. H. Auden, dallied with it

Marxism, however, was never simply a political program in the way that, say socialism or liberalism might be considered such. Like Nazism or fascism, it was rather a comprehensive way of looking at the world. That is why there were attempts at Communist art, Communist architecture, Communist music and literature, and even Communist science, a category mistake if ever there was one. It also transformed understandings of economics, of culture, and, most relevant for our purposes, of history. Indeed, it offered a comprehensive explanatory scheme that not only explained the past but also—crucially—allowed for the prediction in broad terms of the future as well.

Now, at this point I need to issue a disclaimer: Marxism has proved as fissiparous a philosophy as it has a political ideology. As Maoists vied with Stalinists, and Stalinists vied with Trotskyists over arcane details of how and when the transition from one form of society to another would take place and what the necessary conditions were for the radicalization of the proletariat (any who think that the Christian church is uniquely combative over fine points of doctrine have clearly never explored the history of the Marxist Left), so the picture I am going to paint here is necessarily simplified and somewhat impressionistic. My purpose is not to offer an exhaustive account of the varieties of Marxist theory; it is rather to indicate the problems that occur when an explanatory model for history becomes too prescriptive as a means of approaching the subject.

Essentially, Marx's theory of history represented a modification of that proposed by G. W. F. Hegel. Indeed, Marx has been said to have turned Hegel on his head. Hegel's great contribution was to see history as dynamic, as a series of clashing and contradictory forces that continually drove history forward. We could describe this movement of history as a dialectical progression. Hegel's general model of reality starts with an existing element, or thesis, that contains within itself contradictions which unintentionally cause the thesis's opposite, or antithesis. For a time there is a conflict between the two, until a new element, a synthesis emerges. This, in turn, contains its own inner contradictions, and so the process begins anew. Each synthesis is considered an advance on what has gone before because it is closer to the end point or final goal of the process.

One could see how this model could be fruitfully applied in the realm of ideas to the development, for example, of Christian doctrine, say, the doctrine of the Trinity. An emphasis upon the unity of God based upon scriptural teaching in the Old Testament is placed in conflict with the apparent diversity within the Godhead of which the New Testament speaks. In the first three centuries after Christ, unitarian modalism and tritheism stand in antithesis to each other until the church formulates her understanding of the Trinity at the Council of Constantinople in 381. While I would argue that this is a wholly inadequate account of what happened and why, it does at least attempt to offer some explanation for the development beyond "First God was one; then he was plural; finally he was Trinity."

When it came to world history, however, Hegel saw his model as explaining how the world spirit develops gradually into its purest form, until the point of full development where it realizes its own freedom. The dialectic thus defines the movement of history; and it is here that Marx, enamored as a young man with the philosophy of Hegel, made his breakthrough and, to repeat a phrase, turned Hegel on his head. Instead of seeing the dialectic as a metaphysical, spiritual thing, Marx came to see it as a material thing, rooted in the economic conditions of the world. Reality was not spiritual, it was material; and economic circumstances were not the result of spiritual realities but were the basis and foundation of those same realities.

Of course, Marx was not the first to offer an interpretation of the world in primarily material terms; others had done so from the time of the pre-Socratic philosophers. What made Marx's contribution unique was not his materialism but rather two distinctive innovations. First, he made the dramatic claim that all of history could be interpreted in terms of the scheme he offered. In other words, Marx's dialectic was all-consuming, a theory, if you like, of everything; and, as Marxism developed in the twentieth century, it was clear that those who took their cue from him saw this in all of its ramifications, as they developed Marxist theories of everything from fine art to industrial relations to the nature of the family.

Second, he claimed that it was not simply materialism that offered the key to the meaning of history; rather it was a very specific kind of materialism that did so. In line with Hegel, it was *dialectical* materialism, and the key historical manifestation of this dialectic was *class struggle*.

For Marx, history moved through a series of phases, driven by the dialectic of class conflict. Thus, in the Middle Ages, Europe was structured along feudal lines, but eventually feudalism broke down because, over time, it actually fostered the growth of a commercial middle class which undermined the power of the feudal barons. This middle class, the bourgeoisie, would prosper and grow, but eventually the contradictions in its own existence (primarily the drive to squeeze more and more out of those employed to produce the goods upon which it depended for its own well-being, in order to enhance and protect profit margins) would lead it to collapse and to be replaced by the working class, the proletariat, at which point a stage of final material equilibrium would be reached and history, in terms of the dynamic, dialectical forward movement, would come to an end.

That, in very simplistic and broad brushstrokes, was the theory, and even though I am not a Marxist, I acknowledge that it did contain a number of insights. For example, it drew out very clearly the connection between social morality and class structure. Given the material basis of reality and the connection of economic classes, morality functioned as a reflection and a means of reinforcing the values of society as it existed: thus, there was feudal morality, bourgeois morality, and finally there would be communist morality, each determined by the economic framework and conditions. To give an anecdote relative to this, some fifteen or so years ago a Japanese bank failed, and on the British news that night the CEO of said bank appeared in tears, begging forgiveness of his employees and investors. I remember being shocked; had this happened in Britain or the United States, the CEO would be unavailable for comment, only accessible through his lawyers, and would certainly not have made any apologies to his customers or employees, let alone begged for their forgiveness. So why the difference? The Marxist answer would be that Japan moved from feudalism to advanced capitalism so quickly that the morality of the former carried over into the latter because it did not have the prolonged period of modernization that would have eradicated feudal values over time. Thus, as the old samurai lord felt an obligation to protect his people, so the modern Japanese CEO felt the same. His British or American counterparts would not feel or behave the same because the process of modernization was much slower, and the feudal ties had long since been eradicated.

This explanation, like the analysis of the Pliny letter, is a hypothesis and difficult to verify or corroborate; but it has to be acknowledged that the categories of Marxist analysis at least allow us an attempt at explaining why this Japanese CEO's behavior was so much at odds with what one might expect from his Western counterparts. As such it is helpful, interesting, and provocative, and it takes history beyond the boring recitation of names and dates and into the proper historical realm of offering historical explanation for material action. Nevertheless, Marxism contains problems, both in terms of its own history as theory or set of theories, and in terms of its comprehensive claims for its own importance and competence.

In fact, from a fairly early stage, the general theory of class struggle and dialectic was placed under considerable strain. The most obvious practical example would be the Russian Revolution: Russia was a largely peasant-based (and hence feudal) society; the move to proletarian revolution was thus somewhat out of line with the general Marxist theory of political revolution. In fact, the Russian Revolution was led by a middle-class intellectual, Lenin, who theorized that bourgeois intellectuals could radicalize the proletariat and thus, as it were, help the dialectical process along. One might also add China and Cambodia to the list of peasant countries that made the move straight to revolution without developing an advanced bourgeois society as well. This should perhaps have provided a clue that class struggle à la Marxism was not quite the key to history that one might have thought. But more of this later.

From a historian's perspective, Marx's theory offered a grand and, given its comprehensiveness, one might say rather attractive scheme for ordering and interpreting historical events. To use the pretentious technical jargon, it was a metanarrative that attempted to explain everything; and, to its credit, it generated a lot of fascinating examples of historical research and explanation that helped to shape the discipline for over half a century. Yet when we come to look at detailed examples, flaws begin to emerge from which the historian can learn some important general lessons.

Christopher Hill and Seventeenth-Century England

While much Marxist history is weighed down with jargon, is written in barbaric prose, and is dry as dust, the work of Christopher Hill is a notable exception. Like his Marxist contemporary, Eric Hobsbawm, Hill wrote elegant, interesting, and provocative books that were accessible to non-Marxists and nonspecialists. Hill was an Oxford don who spent much of his life both as an active Marxist in political terms and as a historian who specialized in the events surrounding the series of military conflicts of the 1640s, known generally as the English Civil War (even though Scotland and Ireland were also significantly involved). Hill's sympathies are perhaps clear from the fact that, on the day Margaret Thatcher resigned in 1990, he reportedly ran through the quad of his Oxford College crying out, "She is fallen, she is fallen! Babylon the Great is fallen!"

The English Civil War is, without doubt, one of the single most significant periods in British history, among other things profoundly shaping the nature of the monarchy, influencing political theory, facilitating the development of the modern military, transforming the relations of the various parts of the United Kingdom, and witnessing the beginning of England's imperialism. Thus, it is ripe for historical analysis in terms of unpacking its significance on all of these fronts. Most of all, it is, of course, notorious for its climactic moment in the execution of King Charles I. That the "people," in the shape of Parliament, rebelled against the legally constituted monarch and not only brought him to heel but tried him and sent him to the scaffold is a stunning event in history, one at the time seen as having nothing less than eschatological, end-of-time significance. And, as this event by itself clearly reflects something of a social and political revolution, it is ripe for the kind of politically charged analysis that Marxism can offer.

Hill's approach was to see the Civil War in terms of clear class struggle, the classic Marxist approach. Essentially, he argued that it was driven by the middle class (represented by the mainstream Puritans) who wished to curb the power of the monarchy and the feudal lords in order to facilitate the kind of economic activity (essentially trade and nascent capitalism, with its concomitant work and social practices) that would enhance its own influence. The military conflict involved, at least for much of its time, a coalition of the lower classes, generally poor and politically radical, and the middle classes, who were extremely radical in terms of their approach to dismantling feudalism but rather conservative when it came to matters that involved the protection of their class interests over those of their temporary allies among the poor. Thus, according to the narrative, the New Model Army, the military powerhouse of Parliament and the secret of its success in the conflict, drew much of its strength from radicals and from those committed to quasi-democratic ideals; but once the king had been overthrown, this radicalism was curbed and England fell under the sway of a military dictator, Oliver Cromwell, who worked to protect the bourgeois interests of his class.

My own interest in Hill's work derives from the fact that much of his writing focused on the ideology of the English Civil War, that is, the intellectual expressions of the conflict in pamphlets and treatises, particularly those produced by so-called Puritans who, for Hill, represent the winning side in the revolution. Hill is particularly fascinating in this regard because his writing runs counter to what one might expect from a Marxist. Most people, if they know any sayings of Marx at all, know that he declared that "religion is the opium of the people." The meaning of this phrase is relatively straightforward: religion, by offering a rationale for suffering in the present by promising glorious rewards in the afterlife (and sometimes threatening those rewards if rebellion is pursued here on earth), effectively keeps the lower classes in a state of willing subservience.

Of course, events of recent years have shown that this basic thesis is scarcely a universal truth: while religion may on occasion have had such an impact, it is arguable that it was Christian activism in Britain that facilitated the rise of the trade union movement and helped give birth to the Labour Party; more dramatically, no one faced with the rise of militant Islam since the Iranian Revolution of 1979 and atrocities such as 9/11 could be left under any illusion that religion and radical political and social action are antithetical. Indeed, increasingly in the modern world, it is precisely religious conviction that fuels radical politics. And this is what makes Hill's contribution to seventeenth-century studies so interesting, because he, as a Marxist, identified radical Protestantism, both mainstream Puritanism and its more sectarian manifestations, as the source of social and political radicalism in the midcentury, and the Bible, at least for a short period, as a politically revolutionary text. In seventeenth-century England, religion was less akin to opium and more like nitroglycerine, and it was this thesis that Hill explored, using a Marxist class-based analysis as his explanatory scheme.

Numerous examples of Hill's work offer fascinating insights into his approach, but here I will confine myself to just a handful. In *The World Turned Upside Down*, Hill, in typical Marxist fashion, focused on the groups often considered marginal by most historians, at least those historians interested in grand political narrative, intellectual contributions, and macro-economic issues: the illiterate sects, the extremists, and the religious fanatics.[2] His basic argument was that the outlook and ideology of these groups represented the true social radicalism of the 1640s and 1650s. Significantly, the eschatological speculations of these groups, with their expectation of the imminent return of Christ, reflected a world out of joint with itself and undergoing massive social upheaval; and the angst and fear that such times generated manifested itself in radical theological speculation. Class pathologies and class struggle were expressed in a religious, theological idiom. Ultimately, however, the social and economic conditions were not yet ripe for a true proletarian revolution, and they were doomed to failure: in the 1650s, the alliance between the lower and the middle class broke down, as the middle class, epitomized by Cromwell, took firm control, breaking both the nobles and underclass.

Hill's *The English Bible and the Seventeenth-Century Revolution* is in many ways an extension of the kind of argument offered in *The World Turned Upside Down*.[3] Here Hill examines how the Bible itself was used

---

[2]Christopher Hill, *The World Turned Upside Down* (London: Temple Smith, 1972).
[3]Christopher Hill, *The English Bible and the Seventeenth-Century Revolution* (New York: Penguin, 1993).

as a revolutionary handbook, inspiring radicals and social revolutionaries in the seventeenth century, but also how, by the end of that same century, it had lost its power. What we would now call a hermeneutical crisis, by which the Bible had been shown to be susceptible to a whole variety of mutually exclusive readings, effectively robbed it of its dynamism. And in classic Marxist fashion, Hill ends the book by pointing to the fact that the standard English Bible translation was by then the Authorized Version, the result, he argued, of market forces: the theologically and politically more radical Geneva Bible, with its copious notes and illustrations, was simply more expensive to produce and was thus killed off by the very market forces that (according to Hill) Puritan radicalism had helped to unleash. A classic example of Marxist dialectic!

A third, and particularly interesting volume, is Hill's study of John Bunyan, *A Turbulent, Seditious, and Factious People*.[4] Here, Hill addresses the life and literary output of one of the most remarkable men of the seventeenth century: the comparatively uneducated tinker, John Bunyan, who yet produced one of the great literary masterpieces of his—or any other—time, *The Pilgrim's Progress*. Of course, many Christians have read this book as an allegorical description of the life of a believer; but, as a good Marxist, Hill always wants to probe beneath the surface of a text to find out what else might be going on there. And in *Pilgrim's Progress*, he finds a breathtaking critique of the rising capitalism that is reshaping the English landscape—both figuratively and literally.

Before dismissing this latter as some left-wing projectionist fantasy, it is worth reflecting for a moment on his argument. Is it coincidence, for example, that those described by Bunyan as "gentlemen," an avowedly middle-class title, are, within the narrative, typically slimy villains liable to lead the pilgrims astray? And what of Giant Despair? Is he not a landowner who persecutes the homeless pilgrims as they pass by his property? And what is the scene in which the outworkings of sin are most dramatically represented to the reader? Surely it is Vanity Fair, based no doubt on

---

[4]Christopher Hill, *A Turbulent, Seditious, and Factious People* (Oxford: Oxford University Press, 1989).

Bunyan's own experience of such events in real life, and marked by nothing so much as greed manifested in capitalist trading where everything has a price, nothing retains any intrinsic value, and those who disrupt the buying and selling are likely to pay a high price. Looked at in this light, the narrative does not seem quite so straightforward or naïve as perhaps it might otherwise have. In fact, it starts to look decidedly subversive, if not revolutionary, in character. None of this is to claim, of course, that Bunyan was necessarily *conscious* of the anticapitalist polemic that underlay his work; from his perspective he may simply have been drawing on what he had observed of the world around him, a naïve stance of "this is just the way the world is." But Hill wants to bring to our attention that Bunyan's work has political content. Indeed, for Marxists, everything has political content.

The final piece of work I want to mention is not a book but an essay, "The Uses of Sabbatarianism," in the collection entitled *Society and Puritanism in Pre-Revolutionary England.*[5] In this piece, Hill addresses the interesting fact that late sixteenth- and seventeenth-century England and Scotland developed a much more elaborate and strictly enforced view of the Sabbath than was the case in Protestant countries on the continent. The essay is fascinating for a number of reasons, not least because it shows Marxist analysis at its most probing and stimulating; thus, I will spend a little more time teasing out the context and the argument.

The Anglo-Scottish strictness on the issue of the Sabbath is epitomized in the Westminster Larger Catechism's questions 115 to 121. Here, for example, is question and answer 117:

Q: How is the Sabbath or Lord's day to be sanctified?
A: The Sabbath or Lord's day is to be sanctified by an holy resting all the day, not only from such works as are at all times sinful, but even from such worldly employments and recreations as are on other days lawful; and making it our delight to spend the whole time (except so much of it as is to be taken up in works of necessity and mercy) in the public and private

---

[5]Christopher Hill, *Society and Puritanism in Pre-Revolutionary England* (London: Panther, 1969), 141–211.

exercises of God's worship; and to that end, we are to prepare our hearts, and with such foresight, diligence, and moderation, to dispose and seasonably dispatch our worldly business, that we may be the more free and fit for the duties of that day.

This teaching is quite a contrast with medieval Catholicism, early Reformation thinking (William Tyndale and Martin Luther thought Sabbatarianism to be legalism), and even the continental tradition, as exemplified in the Heidelberg Catechism's answer to essentially the same question:

Q. 103: What does God require in the fourth commandment?

A. First, that the ministry of the gospel and the schools be maintained and that, especially on the day of rest, I diligently attend the church of God to hear God's Word, to use the sacraments, to call publicly upon the Lord, and to give Christian offerings for the poor. Second, that all the days of my life I rest from evil works, let the Lord work in me through His Holy Spirit, and so begin in this life the eternal Sabbath.

Even these two brief quotations highlight the difference between the Anglo-Scottish approach and that of the continental Reformed: the former is much more prescriptive about what can and cannot be done; the latter operates at the level of generalities and basic principles; the former legislates for the whole day; the latter simply makes church attendance the overriding priority.

The interesting question is, of course, why the difference? Given the essential commonality of doctrine between continental Reformed churches and their Anglo-Scottish counterparts on so many issues, why is the Sabbath a special case of apparent British exceptionalism? It is the kind of question that good historians love: it is never the norm that has to be explained; it is always the exceptions to the norm.

Sabbatarianism had, in fact, been an issue in the English religious scene since at least the publication of Nicholas Bownd's *The doctrine of the sabbath plainely layde forth* in 1595. Then, with the publication by James I of *The Book of Sports* in 1618 (a guide to various fun activities, such as hunting, which the King thought could and should be pursued on Sunday), views of the Sabbath became a highly politicized part of the struggle between the Crown and the Puritans which culminated, of course, in the very kind of catechetical teaching on the matter noted above in the Westminster Standards.

Thus, one obvious reason for British exceptionalism on this point was the peculiar nature of the religious conflict of the time, and the way this particular issue had functioned within that conflict. But Hill, as a good Marxist, wants to probe deeper and see if there are other reasons that may have led to the conflict, if not made it virtually inevitable. Above all, he wants to drill down below the surface of the social practice to see how it connects to the ongoing struggle of class against class, which drives history along.

To do this, Hill draws the reader's attention to the nature of the medieval church calendar. Medieval Catholicism had two qualities which, among others, made it very successful in the Middle Ages. First, it was very accommodating to folk religion. This point is indisputable. You have a spirit, or a fairy, or even a local god who looks after the village well? No problem. Catholicism can simply replace him/her/it with a patron saint who will do the job just as well, if not better. Indeed, Catholicism's commitment to the developing cult of the saints was surely one of its great strengths during the church's massive expansion during the fourth and fifth centuries, and the winning strategy of a somewhat syncretistic pattern of handling folk religion continued right down until the fifteenth century. Indeed, it is surely not insignificant that witch trials are really a phenomenon of the early modern period, not so much the late medieval; and much of the grassroots tension in Protestantism, at least according to church records, was generated not by pastoral problems related to Catholicism (e.g., parishioners sneaking off to attend Mass) but by folk religion (e.g., parishioners casting spells to make milkmaids fall in love with them).[6]

The second quality was that Catholicism built its church calendar in terms of an annual rhythm determined by the agrarian nature of the Euro-

---

[6] An excellent study of parish records relative to such cases is Margo Todd, *The Culture of Protestantism in Early Modern Scotland* (Yale: Yale University Press, 2002).

pean economy in the Middle Ages. Feast days—and there were plenty of them—were generally timed for points in the year when there was not much to be done. Thus, Christmas came in the bleak midwinter, when there was neither any sowing nor any reaping to do. One could scarcely have had such a big celebration at a time when the seed needed to be laid in the ground, or the crops needed to be gathered before the autumn storms arrived or the first frost of the year occurred. In short, the calendar reflected the kind of life upon which a feudal economy was built. In fact, one could go even further than that: the calendar formalized and reinforced—even articulated—the rhythm of life upon which the way of life depended.

This rhythm came under strain almost from the start of the Reformation. Indeed, if the Lutheran revolution started in 1517 with the nailing on a chapel door of an advertisement for that most medieval of things, a university debate, the Zurich Reformation started in 1522 with the refusal of a printer, Christoph Froschauer, to make his men abide by the rules of the Lenten fast. Instead, he gathered them together to enjoy a good sausage, with the Reformer, Huldrych Zwingli, present, though not a partaker of the feast. Froschauer's reason? His men's work required that they be well fed. The point is clear: the work practices of those in urban economies based upon trade and production are significantly different from those of people in rural communities where agriculture is the primary industry. The latter are dependent upon the rhythm of the seasons; the former are more independent of these factors. The one has labor patterns determined by the crop cycle; the other has labor patterns determined by the nature of production and trade.

One does not have to be a Marxist, or even a materialist, to see the connection between religious practice and economic activity here. Strict Sabbatarianism would be impossible to enforce in a rural economy where it may well be that crops have to be gathered on a Sunday to store the grain in a barn before an impending storm arrives; and the kind of year that allows for long periods of inactivity, so typical of agrarian societies, would not suit a printer who needs to make sure that five hundred copies of a particular book are printed, bound, and delivered to a shop by a certain date, perhaps in the very middle of winter.

Thus, in asking the fascinating question, why do England and Scotland develop a highly elaborate and strict form of Sabbatarianism in the late sixteenth and seventeenth centuries, Hill's answer is: it is part of the ideology of the class that is rising to dominance at that point, the bourgeoisie, whose power lies in production, distribution, and trade. In this context, Sabbatarianism embodies precisely those economic virtues that drive this kind of economy: a regular, weekly work pattern, with regular, weekly periods of rest. Further, Sabbatarianism is more than just a religious expression of these values; it is also a means of social control. Sabbatarianism is the bourgeoisie's means of giving its work ethic a divine sanction. It effectively justifies its own work practices (and, incidentally, makes agrarian work practices naturally look inferior and less godly), and enforces them: if God is a Sabbatarian, how can such a practice be opposed by, say, the working class, since it represents the divine, objective order, with very real eternal consequences attached to it?[7] Opium of the people, anyone?

Thus, Hill explains Anglo-Scottish exceptionalism on this issue by pointing to the exceptionally advanced nature of the British economy in comparison to the rest of Europe at this time. The Sabbath issue is connected to the rise of the middle class. And, in this context, the pushing of the *Book of Sports* by James I and then his son, Charles I, can be seen as an attempt by the old feudal order to reassert its own ideology. In other words, the Sabbath controversies come down to class warfare, a classic Marxist analysis of a historical situation.

Given all of this, what are we to make of Christopher Hill's contribution? A number of points come immediately to mind. First, and positively, Hill is using his Marxist framework as a means of *explaining* what is going on in history. As noted above, history is more than the simple listing of events or actions; it involves the construction of a narrative that seeks to

---

[7]It is tempting here to extend Hill's analysis to the present day and to see the collapse of Sabbatarianism as also precipitated by economic considerations. Once economies shift from production to consumption, then the idea of a day each week when there can be no consumption is not simply an anachronism, it is a profound inconvenience and must be abolished as soon as possible. This is exactly what happened in Britain in the 1980s, as the economic revolution under Margaret Thatcher took place, despite some (initially successful) opposition from churches and (ironically, at least for a Marxist) trade unionists.

connect and to explain how events relate to each other. This Hill typically did in an exemplary fashion: the English Civil War was not simply a random collection of military skirmishes fought between armies that just happened to be wandering around the English countryside in the 1640s. It had a significance and a rationale which Hill has attempted to explore using the principles of a Marxist analysis.

Second, Hill refuses simply to take the accounts of the protagonists at face value. One commonplace of historians is the need for some chronological distance from events and actions; this is because the whole issue of historical perspective is significant. Individual actors in a historical drama may not actually have as deep an understanding of the events in which they are involved as a later historian with access to more documentation. Further, individual motives can often be virtually irrelevant in understanding great historical events. We now know, for example, that many of those who signed up to fight in the American Civil War did not do so because of some deep-seated commitment for or against slavery or even States' rights; more often than not, local, mundane factors carried a whole lot more weight—"My best friends all signed up so I did too" would be one such example of reasoning. But that does not mean we can explain the American Civil War simply on the basis of neighborhood relationships or the loyalty involved in local friendships. This is where Hill is again strong: he attempts to explain massive historical actions and events in terms of larger causal factors.

Third, we can also give Hill credit for moving beyond the narrow range of palace politics to explain the English Civil War. He did this in two ways: first, he looked at economic patterns as providing the basic structures for historical movement; and, second, he took seriously many of those groups that were typically marginalized by traditional "top down" historians, who tended to privilege the thoughts and deeds of elite individuals or groups and ignore those at the bottom of the social scale—even though, economically and often militarily, this was where the raw manpower lay. In this, Hill is an early exemplar of the kind of history (such as African-American, feminist, etc.) which, despite frequent excess, has often produced fascinating insights into historical movements and meaning that will never feature in historical explanations based purely on examination of the social and cultural elite.

Yet there are also a number of difficulties in Hill's approach. The first is one that is always problematic for the historian committed to a particularly precise philosophy of history: the limited nature of the questions asked. If it is assumed at the outset as a scientific fact that history is the unfolding of class struggle, and that everything, from the organization of labor to the writing of a poem, ultimately has historical meaning and significance only because of its relationship to this struggle, then the only questions that are going to be asked, or that are seen as significant, are those that are shaped by this very philosophy. To take a facetious example: if I believe that history is really a function of the color of ladies' hats on display in a certain shop window on Main Street, then, whatever happens in that town, the questions I ask as a historian are going to run along the lines of, "And what color hats were on display when the council passed the parking legislation, or when inflation climbed to twenty percent, or when the local bus drivers went on strike?" The question imposes a form of reality on the historical phenomena that may blind me to other, more significant factors (for example, whether the council's parking legislation was influenced by a record of accidents on that particular stretch of road). Thus, the Marxist with class struggle on his mind will always ask questions of the evidence that reflect this basic presupposition. Such questions can contain within themselves the potential for distorted answers, and may also blind me to evidence that simply does not fit the categories within which I am operating.

This takes me back to my earlier point: historians need to be aware of the explanatory schemes with which they operate and need to hold to them as heuristic devices or as hypotheses that are themselves open to correction or modification in light of the evidence. To go back to an example from the last chapter, I may have a theory that nobody was gassed at Auschwitz but that all the Jews were transported to Madagascar; but I must then go and see if the evidence supports this claim or not, and, if it does not, I must change my hypothesis in a way that takes account of the evidence.

The second, most obvious—and surely the most lethal—problem is the question of the falsifiability of Hill's claims. This was the Achilles' heel of

Marxist theory in general, as pointed out with devastating effect by the philosopher Karl Popper in his little book, *The Poverty of Historicism*; Popper also drew parallels between Marxism and Darwinism, which he saw as vulnerable to the same criticism.[8] For Popper, the problem with Marxism was that it was a theory that presented itself as scientific fact but which was unable to meet one of the most basic criteria of scientific knowledge: falsifiability. In short, the question Popper wanted to ask was, under what conditions would it be possible to disprove any of Marxism's basic claims? The answer is: none.

If true, this makes Marxism fundamentally unscientific as an approach to the past. More than that, it means it is ultimately immune to criticism because there is no criticism from outside that it will accept as legitimate. Now, historians never operate as blank pages. As we read texts or examine artifacts, there is a certain engagement of the imagination. Based on our knowledge of how language works, we begin to construct frameworks by which we understand a certain piece of writing. From our knowledge of other aspects of the world, we work by analogy to produce models that connect the dots between one piece of evidence and another; we even develop criteria by which one thing is seen as a piece of evidence while another thing we judge irrelevant, or by which we prioritize certain types of evidence over certain others. In all of this, however, one thing is crucial to good historical method: as we develop a thesis or a theory or an interpretation of a piece of evidence, we need to look for other evidence that will refute, undermine, or cause us to revise the said thesis.

Thus, if I have a series of romantic letters in front of me written in the early twentieth century by a man, Ronald Smith, to a woman, Clare Jones, I might start to put together a certain hypothesis: these are written by a young man in love with a young girl. The difference in surname indicates they are not married, so perhaps this is a common-or-garden romance between two young people with a view to marriage. As I read on, Ronald makes reference to another woman, Julie Smith, from whom he desires to keep the relationship a secret. At this point, perhaps, I hypothesize that

---

[8]Karl R. Popper, *The Poverty of Historicism* (New York: Basic Books, 1960).

what I am reading about is an illicit affair between a married man and his mistress, with Julie Smith being the victim of his cheating. Yet there are other possibilities. Marriage is not the only reason why they might share the same name: Julie Smith might be his sister, or mother, or cousin, any of whom might have personal reasons for disapproving of the relationship between Ronald and Clare. Thus, in order to argue my historical interpretation—that this is an illicit affair—I need to track down further evidence. Positive evidence might come in the form of a marriage certificate for Ronald and Julie that predates the correspondence and this would help to verify my theory; evidence that would falsify the theory might include birth certificates for Ronald and Julie, indicating their relationship is one of consanguinity rather than marriage. If such documents come to light, then they immediately confirm my thesis or falsify it and cause me to revise it somewhat. If I can find neither, then modesty requires that I present my theory accordingly, as a plausible interpretation given the current state of my knowledge but in no way as a definitive statement of the matter. Thus, I state my case as one built on circumstantial evidence, but being clear to all that my thesis is at best provisional. The important thing is that I am aware of the type of evidence that would render my thesis valid or invalid, and until I can definitively produce the former or exclude the latter, I cannot claim to be presenting the rock-solid truth about the relationship.

One could even strengthen this and say that it is actually the duty of a historian, when he postulates a certain thesis or interpretation of particular phenomena, to make a special effort to find evidence that would call his theory into question. If I am arguing for the idea that Lee Harvey Oswald acted alone when he assassinated John F. Kennedy, I should take special care to look at anything that might suggest a wider conspiracy: his time in the Soviet Union; his links to American Communists; whether he had ties to Cuba, etc. Such is basic to good historical method.

This, of course, brings us back to Christopher Hill and his Marxist read of the seventeenth century. Now the reader, mesmerized by my account of how Hill applies Marxist analysis to the English Civil War, might at this point be reaching for his methodological machine gun, just itching to shoot me down: surely, you say, if we can demonstrate that, say, the upper classes were deeply involved on the Puritan side of things in the war, then would that not constitute the kind of evidence that would falsify the Marxist thesis? Thus, the presence or absence of this class on this side in this war would enable Marxism to meet Popper's criteria of falsifiability, would it not? One might think so, but in so thinking, one would also betray one's ignorance of Marxist thought.

One important aspect of Marxist philosophy is the notion of *false consciousness*. Essentially, this is the idea that economic classes can actually be tricked into identifying the interests of another class with their own, a form, if you like, of mass psychosis or delusion. A good example (provided to me by a Marxist friend) might be the British National Health Service. In Britain, it is a virtually unquestioned orthodoxy that there should be some level of universal healthcare for all, paid for via taxation. This would seem to be of great benefit to those too poor to be able to pay for their own health insurance costs if they lived, for example, under the American system of private health provision. And yet, my Marxist friend would tell you that the NHS, like the Welfare State as a whole, is one giant capitalist con trick: by promising care and providing a minimal amount of subsistence, these institutions fool the poor into thinking that society (run, at this point, by the capitalist bourgeoisie) cares for them and has their best interests at heart; in other words, it is actually just another form of political opium, helping to defuse the class struggle, delay the collapse of capitalism, and thus stall the rise to dominance of the working class. For this reason, my friend would argue that true Marxists in Britain should vote Conservative: only the Tories will dismantle the Welfare State, drive the contradictions of capitalism to their logical conclusion, and hasten the glorious day of the workers' revolution.

So much for my friend's nonsense. What has this to do with Marxist philosophies of history? Well, simply this: if you find that the whole of the English Civil War was led by the aristocracy, if every tract penned by Parliament argued for a return to medieval feudalism and every poor soldier who enlisted did so because he thought the King just needed to have his enthusiasm for church ritual redirected, it would do no damage at all to Hill's interpretation because it could all be dismissed as so many instances of false consciousness. All of these different groups and authors could have been suffering from delusion and so nothing you say to the contrary can do any damage to the basic thesis that what is going on is class warfare. Positive evidence (such as Bunyan's typical characterization of wicked people as "gentlemen") serves to prove the thesis; counterevidence, such as the involvement of the feudal nobility in support of the Parliamentary cause, simply indicates the depth at which false consciousness is capable of alienating people from their class interests. In other words, the grid for historical interpretation is more than something that facilitates the selection and interpretation of evidence: it offers an all-encompassing aprioristic view of reality into which the phenomena of history must be made to fit, whether by fair means or foul. It is a form of idealism that will ultimately squeeze the particulars of history into a presupposed framework that is derived from abstract philosophical principles, not the result of induction or deduction from historical phenomena.

One could perhaps say that Marxist theory at this level represents a rather sophisticated conspiracy theory. Anyone who has spent any time on the Internet will have come across the various bizarre theories that lurk there, whether relating to the alleged death of Paul McCartney, the alleged survival of Elvis, or the existence of various arcane groups who really control the world's governments. One of the problems with such theories is that any evidence one provides to counter them or refute them is, to the theory's adherents, merely more evidence of just how deep the conspiracy runs. You find DNA from the grave that matches that of Elvis? Well that simply shows that the undertakers or the DNA laboratory are also involved in the conspiracy. In the same way, you claim you can demonstrate that many members of the upper class were fighting the king in the Civil War? Well, that just shows how confused they were over their own class interests.

Ironically, as regards Hill, I saw this flaw most dramatically (and tragically) in a BBC documentary some years ago. The program was examining the fascination of British intellectuals, such as George Bernard Shaw, with Stalin and communism in the 1930s, and how the Soviet leader had invited numbers of them, including Shaw and Hill, to travel through

101

the Soviet Union to see the Communist utopia in all of its glory. Like coal mines whitewashed before a royal visit, one can only imagine how stage-managed and choreographed such tours were, and how closely they resembled real life for the typical Soviet citizen. By the time of the documentary, of course, Shaw was long since dead; but Hill was still alive, an aging Marxist academic, living in the aftermath not simply of the 1930s show trials, but also the revelations about the gulags, the 1956 Hungarian Uprising, the Prague Spring, the erection and demolition of the Berlin Wall, and, of course, the collapse of the Soviet Union in the early 1990s. That is quite a tally of evidence which, one would think, might militate against the idea that Stalin's Russia was a worker's paradise, the utopian synthesis at the end of the dialectical materialist rainbow. Thus, I was eager to hear Hill's comments on his time in Russia from the vantage point of the post-Soviet world.

Finally, the moment came for the question: the interviewer asked Hill, what about the famines caused by Stalin's economic policies in the 1930s? I will never forget the great historian's answer: there were no famines. What about all the evidence? responded the somewhat startled interviewer. There is no evidence, said Hill, and any that you claim to be able to provide is merely the manufactured misinformation of those imperialist Westerners who wish to hide the glories of what communism has done and can do.

The answer was stunning because Hill was an Oxford historian, a man who made his living by interpreting the past on the basis of empirical evidence. What it showed was that his commitment to Marxist philosophy trumped his commitment to allowing the evidence to shape his thinking; indeed, when push came to shove, his Marxism led him to sound as delusional as the typical black helicopter aficionado from the craziest corners of the virtual world. On this point, at least, there appeared little—indeed, there was no—difference between Hill and the typical Holocaust denier. They simply came from different ends of the political spectrum.

In the years since Hill's heyday, seventeenth-century scholars have demonstrated that the whole model of class warfare simply does not do justice to the complexities of the English, Scottish, and Irish conflicts of the 1640s and 1650s. There has been a resurgence of interest in the nature of court politics leading up to the Civil War, as in the work of John Adamson, whose book, *The Noble Revolt: The Overthrow of Charles I*, examines the conflict from the perspective of struggles between vested interest in Parliament and the Crown.[9] Then, the work of men such as Conrad Russell and John Morrill has placed back at the center of the narrative religious considerations, seeing the conflict not so much as the first modern bourgeois revolution as the last medieval war of religion. Yet to a Marxist, all this debunking is itself so much bunkum, mere examples of highly sophisticated false consciousness—both of the seventeenth century and of the modern scholars themselves—which is incapable of getting to the truth.

At this point, Marxism is problematic because, in its nonfalsifiability, it ceases to be a heuristic device, useful for selecting and interpreting evidence, and is more of an all-embracing ideology, a Procrustean bed, an *a priori* system that simply discounts or reinterprets any evidence that might call its fundamental veracity into account. So how can it be of use to historians?

I would suggest that the fundamental problem with Marxism is precisely this lack of interpretative modesty, the fact that it presents itself as a complete picture of reality and thus as capable of providing an exhaustive account of that same reality. There would seem little doubt, for example, that there are real social and economic tensions in *The Pilgrim's Progress* of a kind that a Marxist frame of reference helps to bring to the surface. The pious Christian reader is likely to miss these entirely, taking the work at face value as an allegory of the Christian life and never asking why Bunyan chose to portray aspects of that life in the specific way that he did. Yet it is a giant philosophical leap to move from seeing such tensions as reflected in the book to arguing that the historical significance of the work can ultimately be explained in terms of categories that track back to the single point of class warfare, or the varying degrees of true and false consciousness that the work demonstrates. Class is undoubtedly a factor in history; but to make it the ultimate factor is to impose upon history a

---

[9]John Adamson, *The Noble Revolt: The Overthrow of Charles I* (London: Weidenfeld & Nicolson, 2007).

grid that narrows the historian's focus and requires various acts of intellectual gymnastics.

Two recent histories brought this point—the oversimplification involved in Marxist theory, albeit often expressed in very subtle and complex ways—home to me. One is Niall Ferguson's *The War of the World* , a study of the various revolutions and military conflicts of the twentieth century.[10] Central to Ferguson's narrative is the idea of nation and ethnicity. Indeed, contra the classic Marxist theories of why the twentieth century was so blood-soaked, Ferguson argues that it is not class interests that drove the various wars, but ethnic conflict. From Turkey's massacre of Armenians in 1815 to the Rape of Nanking to the Holocaust to the Balkans to Rwanda, Ferguson's point is that it was tribalism, nationalism, and racism that provided the real causes of conflict. To put it simply, people have a preference for other people who look like them, sound like them, have the same values and beliefs as them, and have the same basic identity in terms of background and history as them; and this creates problems when different groups come into contact with each other, competing for land resources and the like.

The second history is *Comrades* by Robert Service, a world history of communism.[11] Service tells the story of communism from Marx through to the present day, but one of the things that emerges in the work, almost by accident as it is not really one of Service's own foci, is the level at which ethnicity operated within the movement. Whether it is Stalin's own racist attitudes, even toward his own Georgian people, or the way in which the violence of the Cambodian revolution actually broke down along ethnic lines, the role of ethnicity is once again a significant detail in the story. Reading these two books within a short time of each other raised for me the acute question: while Marxism would typically have regarded racism as either false consciousness or another idiom for expressing the class struggle, is it possible that the roles are really to be reversed, that Marxism has more often than not actually been an idiom for expressing racial, ethnic, or national interests and concerns?

---

[10]Niall Ferguson, *The War of the World* (New York: Allen Lane, 2006).

[11]Robert Service, *Comrades!* (Cambridge, MA: Harvard University Press, 2007).

One might add to this the recent resurgence of militant Islam. While original Marxist theory regarded religion as a pacifier, as the opium of the people, events since the Iranian Revolution of 1979 have not simply challenged this view, they have effectively shattered it. Far from making people into docile, if not supine, conformist members of society, religion can mobilize large numbers of people to violent action, and the promise of eternal life need not short-circuit political activism but can rather inspire a suicide bomber.

Again, all of these can no doubt be dismissed by Marxists with a wave of the hand as examples of false consciousness, but, one can respond by saying that that is a claim which stands above and beyond the reach of the historical evidence. Additionally, it is vulnerable to immanent critique along lines that have left the Left hopelessly compromised. As mentioned earlier, classic Marxist theory sees history as determined by class conflict, and thus as moving inexorably from feudalism to capitalism to communism as the inherent contradictions in each of the earlier phases bring about the move to the future. What the Iranian Revolution represented, and, even more explicitly the Taliban takeover of Afghanistan, was, in Marxist categories, a return to a form of feudalism. Now, Marxist theorists had debated long and hard as to how the dialectic works out precisely in history, and they had managed somehow to explain the fact that the most notable communist revolutions—those in Russia and China—took place in societies that were arguably very feudal in structure, contradicting the idea that advanced industrial capitalism was a necessary precondition of such. But the triumph of the Taliban represented not simply an anomaly in the timetabling of dialectical materialism; it was actually a fundamental reversal of the process. It is arguable that in his work on the seventeenth century, Hill anticipated the revolutionary force of religious belief and offered a necessary corrective to the naïvely received wisdom of earlier Marxists; but not even he would have anticipated the reversal of the inexorably forward moving dialectic of history.[12]

---

[12]One might also add that it also destroys the theory of conservative Hegelian historian, Francis Fukuyama, who saw the collapse of the Soviet Union as signaling the end of history: with the triumph of Western capitalist democracies, the historical process had come to an end and resolved its dialectical tensions, and there was nothing left to do but sit back and watch the spread of free markets and democracy across the globe. The problem is, of course, that he failed to anticipate the resurgence (or resilience) of religious militancy, of tribalism, and of nationalism. History at the start of the twenty-

I am not one of those who regarded the demolition of the Berlin Wall, the execution of the Ceausescus, and the dismantling of the Soviet Union as signaling the death of Marxism as an analytical theory. Practically, Marxist Communism appears impossible to realize in terms of a political state or a pattern of social and economic organization; but the truth of Marxist theory, as a means of analyzing society and predicting, in broad terms, the shape of the future never depended on the success of the Soviet Union. Nevertheless, I do believe that, even as an analytical theory, Marxism as a philosophy of history should be dead. Partly this is the result of the methodological flaw it embodies, as epitomized in the idea of false consciousness, a concept that essentially renders it invulnerable to criticism and makes it an elaborate and sophisticated form of conspiracy theory; partly it is the result of a vast array of empirical evidence that would seem to point to other factors, such as ethnicity, as being of significance—even, ironically, in the history of organized communism itself; and partly it is on the grounds that history itself, in terms of the resurgence of religion, combined with a move back toward feudalism, flies in the face of Marxism's most precious tenet: the dialectical forward moving nature of history.[13]

Conclusion

Historians identify and interpret evidence, and, on the basis of this, construct narratives. This is a complex business because human historical actions are themselves always complex and impossible to reduce to single causes, intentions, or motivations. In this context, it is important to realize that forces far larger than any individual agent are at play in the world,

---

first century looks far from being at an end. Historians should do what they do best—interpreting the past—and avoid that which they typically do very badly—predicting the future. For Fukuyama, see his *The End of History and the Last Man* (New York: Free Press, 2006).

[13]Part of the chaos created for Marxists by the Taliban and company is the strange set of alliances that have emerged on the political Left. To Marx, it would have been obvious that, in the struggle with feudalism, one should back capitalism, if for no other reason than the fact that it represents a more advanced form of social organization and should always win in a particular struggle with feudalism. The typical reaction of the Left to the wars in Afghanistan and Iraq has, however, been one of condemnation of the efforts of the West. In saying this, I am neither speaking for or against the West in these conflicts; I am simply observing the strange anomaly of the Left backing reactionary feudalism against advanced capitalism.

and that human beings are not simply shaped by what they read or what they hear, but also by hidden forces of which they themselves might be unaware, such as economic and ethnic factors.

Grand interpretative schemes such as Marxism have proved helpful, historically, in offering frameworks by which to make sense of the chaos that is so often the first impression the historian has when looking at the artifacts of history. What qualifies as evidence? How does it fit together? What are the grand themes of history? All these questions are answered by the great theories of history, of which Marxism is perhaps the foremost recent example.

The danger comes when the theory becomes less a means of penetrating history and more a prescriptive, Procrustean bed into which the evidence must fit or be twisted to fit. To be sure, we do well to acknowledge the power of economic and material forces in influencing human thought and behavior, but we also need to be wary of reducing human beings and history to a sound bite, however sophisticated it may be. Class struggle is helpful in understanding some events, but clearly inappropriate in addressing others; ethnic conflict also helps us to gain insight into some matters and not others. The important thing for a historian is that a balance be maintained between an *a priori* model that allows an identification and interrogation of evidence, and an acknowledgment that the evidence itself may require a modification or even an ultimate rejection of the model. The denial by Christopher Hill that there were ever famines in Russia should be a salutary warning that all historians, however talented, need to be aware of how their own ideological commitments, left unchecked, can lead to ridiculous and, in some circumstances, downright sinister places.

CHAPTER 3

The Past Is a Foreign Country

One of the greatest temptations for historians, particularly perhaps for historians studying the history of ideas, is to impose on the past ideas, categories, or values that were simply nonexistent or that did not have the same function or significance during the time being studied. The roots of the problem are obvious: we live in the present; the objects of historical study relate to the past; and as L. P. Hartley famously quipped at the beginning of *The Go-Between*, "The past is a foreign country; they do things differently there." Indeed, the analogy with a foreign country is a helpful one: anybody who has spent any time living abroad in a strange country will know that not only can the language be difficult to understand, but social conventions can appear very strange and incomprehensible as well. The only way to overcome these problems is to spend time learning the language, the dialects, and the manners of the place.

For the historian, the problem of anachronism can take a number of different forms. For example, it could be that in reading a particular text, the historian fails to understand that the meaning of a word has changed over time, and thus he imposes a meaning on the text that was never there. A good example might be the term *liberty*. Living at the start of the twenty-first century in a liberal democracy, I am inclined to understand this word in terms of self-determination, lack of government interference in my life, the right to live and work where I choose, the right to vote, the right to spend my money as I wish, the right to pursue whatever religion I want, etc. In other words, the term is a hallmark of the modern democratic mindset, focused on the individual. In the seventeenth century, however, prior to John Locke and certainly prior to Thomas Jefferson, the term was used by, among others, Presbyterians such as Samuel Rutherford: when he uses it, he means it to refer to the freedom of the church to govern itself, not to the democratic freedom of the individual to be self-determining. Indeed, the last thing on Rutherford's mind would have been liberty in regard to religious practices, for to allow other religions or even other forms of Christianity besides Reformed Presbyterianism would in Rutherford's mind have involved the government in the toleration of idolatry and idolaters that would have incurred the wrath of God.

A second form of anachronism is one that sees the past's agenda simply in terms of modern developments. Again, the notion of *liberty* provides a good example: we can go back and read the past simply as one long story that culminates in the values we hold and thus which legitimates them, as if we stand at the end of history and all that has gone before has been part of one great, inexorable movement toward the ever-better, ever-more-enlightened present. OK, we might say, Rutherford did not hold to liberty as Jefferson did or as we ourselves do, but in arguing for the restriction of the power of the state in internal matters of church discipline, confession, and liturgy, Rutherford was nonetheless moving in a direction that leads to modern liberal democracy. Thus, Rutherford becomes significant not so much for what he did in his own day or the way in which he connects to the past, but rather as a harbinger of things to come. This can lead to the temptation for us to ask of the past only those questions which seem to be significant in the world of today and perhaps to ignore the many other potential pathways or streams of ideas that ultimately went nowhere but that, in their time, were very significant and could easily have triumphed.

A third form of anachronism is what I call categorical anachronism, by which I mean the use of a particular category as a means of analyzing a historical phenomenon, but where the category is not really appropriate to the time and place under discussion. Anti-Semitism is one such category, which we will look at in more detail below. Suffice it to say at this point that it is a *racial* category and thus relevant to analysis of societies and individuals who think in racial terms. This really means that, by and large, it is not appropriate when discussing events and actions prior to the nineteenth century.

Another example of categorical anachronism would be nationalism. This is really a function of nation-states, and the nation-state as we know it really emerged in the nineteenth century as part of the post-Napoleonic restructuring of Europe. Indeed, in the case of Germany, we might even go as late as Bismarck's policies of the 1860s and 1870s before we can talk meaningfully about the German nation and German nationalism and thereby mean something analogous to what we might mean by the idea today. This should temper the way we talk about, say, Martin Luther. In much of his writing in 1519–1521, he will make great play of his German-ness and never miss an opportunity to take a swipe at the Italians. Yet there was no Germany in the sense of a nation at that time, only a collection of territories that formed the Holy Roman Empire; nor was there an Italy in the sense of a single political entity. Luther was aware of linguistic and geographical issues that united him to some and divided him from others, and he was no doubt also acutely aware of the geography of politics at the time; but to think of him as a German nationalist or patriot would be anachronistic. He had no nation-state by which to define his identity, nor any country named Germany of which he could be proud.

Another form of anachronism is that of the imposition of moral, ethical, or intellectual standards which did not apply during the time being studied. A good example from church history might be the status of the doctrine of the Trinity. In a class I teach each year on early Christianity, Christians who believe that the truth never changes often ask whether the

Greek Apologists, for example, believed in the Trinity as expressed in the Nicene Creed. That is an anachronistic question: the Nicene Creed (really the Creed of Constantinople) was not formulated until AD 381, but the Greek Apologists lived in the second century. Thus to hold them to creedal standards that were not operative in their time is an act of anachronism. It is the equivalent of asking whether Mississippi bluesman, Robert Johnson, was a fan of the Rolling Stones. His music may have had potent connections to the early Stones material and influenced it profoundly, and indeed it may be that the Stones could not have been the Stones without his prior contribution, but he was dead long before Mick Jagger and Keith Richards were singing nursery rhymes, let alone rhythm and blues.

A good literary example of anachronism is the novel *Old Mortality* by Sir Walter Scott. In this book, set in the covenanting times in Scotland, the young covenanting hero, Henry Morton, finds himself caught between loyalty to his cause and love for a lady who is connected to his opponents. Throughout the novel, he is portrayed as an advocate of religious tolerance and thus as vexed and perplexed by the factionalism of the religious radicals around him. He is, in fact, of a kind that was really very typical of the era in which Sir Walter Scott lived and of whom Scott approved, but which was certainly not in evidence during the actual period of time that the author claims to be portraying. In other words, the novel presents us with nineteenth-century values of tolerance being advocated by a late seventeenth-century man, a clear case of anachronism. Scott's novel is great entertainment, but it embodies a romantic view of the past and really gives very little insight into how the Covenanters and their enemies actually thought and why they acted in the way they did.

Now, Scott's work is fiction and claims only a loose relationship to the past, but the problem with anachronism is that the potential for this error is an ever-present reality for the historian who wishes to do something more with the past than use it merely as the context for a fictional story. Any attempt at writing history must of necessity bring the horizon of the historian and his own time, place, and context to bear on the horizon of the past. I cannot write and think as a sixteenth-century man because I am not one, and the world in which I live is not the sixteenth-century world. I have a perspective on the sixteenth century that is shaped by my own historical situation, by intervening events, and by a modern knowledge of the world. Indeed, surely this is one of the great strengths of history writing, in that it involves a synthesis of data, with the benefit of chronological hindsight, that allows us to offer not simply robotic chronologies of who did what and where, but of why they acted in the way they did and what significance their actions had. Yet this is the very point at which anachronism can rear its head: to undertake this task of history means that the *present* must engage with the past, and in doing so, there is always a danger that anachronistic ideas from the present will creep into the analysis in ways that are unhelpful and that ultimately run counter to the evidence.

Given this, I would suggest that, in part, the problem of anachronism is a problem of degree. All history is going to be anachronistic in one sense, since all history is written with the benefit of hindsight. Take, for example, one of the key events leading up to the Second World War. In 1938, the infamous "Munich Agreement" was greeted in Britain as a major diplomatic triumph: it sacrificed Czechoslovakia to Nazi imperial ambitions, but appeared to secure "peace in our time," to use Neville Chamberlain's infamous phrase, and was greeted in Britain with something of a collective sigh of relief. We now know that Neville Chamberlain's trip to Munich in 1938 ultimately failed to prevent the Second World War, because we can see (as Chamberlain did not) that Hitler never regarded the agreement as anything more than a mere paper promise, to be ignored as soon as was convenient. Interpreting Munich in light of Hitler's later invasion of Poland, the Second World War as a whole and, indeed, the Holocaust, is anachronistic in the broadest sense of the word: it interprets earlier events in terms of later events, and sets an order and teleology to the story that was not clear at the time and that certainly runs counter to the intention of Hitler and Chamberlain when they signed, since the former did not believe the British would ever fight, and the latter thought the agreement would contain Nazi expansionism. But such "anachronism" is still historically very helpful and appropriate, since the intentions of Hitler and the miscalculations of the British and French governments in 1938 are clear in hindsight in a way that they were not so earlier. The evidence allows us—

indeed, requires us—to approach the topic in this way. Alternatives—that Hitler was the hapless dupe of ruthless generals; that he never intended to invade Poland; that he had no ambitions beyond Czechoslovakia at the time of signing the agreement—can all be shown to be fallacious by looking at the subsequent actions of the Fuehrer and his military high command. This involves bringing later knowledge and perspective to bear on earlier events; but, in cases such as this, this later knowledge fulfills a heuristic function, enabling us to understand more clearly what exactly is going on in the earlier period of time.

It is, of course, not necessary to assume that hindsight demands only one particular interpretation of the evidence. We saw in chapter 1 that there are Holocaust historians who are functionalists, regarding the evidence as indicating the evolution of the Holocaust plan over time, and those who are intentionalists, regarding it as the Nazi plan from very early on in the Third Reich. Both schools inevitably interpret earlier events in light of later actions and offer an explanatory account of what happened, which they see to be consistent with the evidence. Yet there comes a point where the normal logic of historical study involving such hindsight ceases, where the "benefit of hindsight" no longer has what we might call a heuristic function and becomes rather more distorting in the way it approaches the subject. To reduce the above example of the Munich Agreement to absurdity: if we were to read the events of Munich, 1938, in a way that saw them as part of a self-conscious move on Hitler's part to facilitate the London Blitz, that would, I suggest, involve anachronism in the way that later events are read back into earlier events in an act of radical eisegesis. Certainly the events at Munich form part of the network of actions and events that will lead to the Blitz, but to take the orders that ensured the latter and make them part of the self-conscious Nazi strategy at Munich is to fly in the face of the evidence and to indulge in anachronism: the evidence we have suggests that Hitler was banking on British weakness in the face of his aggression on mainland Europe, that his concern was always living space (*Lebensraum*) in an ethnically-cleansed eastern Europe, and that war with Britain was actually an unanticipated consequence of Hitler's foreign policy.

Thus, to argue that Munich was part of a strategy to legitimate the bombing of London is an absurd, anachronistic distortion that is contradicted by the evidence. It is an example of the *post hoc, propter hoc* fallacy that holds that simply because one event occurred after another, then the former caused the latter (I address this more in the final chapter). Unlike the debate between functionalists and intentionalists regarding the Holocaust, there is no evidence to connect the earlier Munich Agreement and the later Blitz in the way proposed.

Given this, the question is, how can one spot this kind of problem and how does one avoid it? To begin with, it is worth making the general point that the question of anachronism is ultimately once again one of the self-conscious method of the historian. As this statement implies, a significant part of the solution to the problem is thus to be *self-conscious* about historical method, about how one is reading the evidence, and to appreciate the fact that one is engaging with a different time and a different place. If one does this, then one is more likely to be aware that there is, therefore, a danger of slipping into one of the fallacies associated with anachronism. Simply to be aware of the potential problem is a crucial move toward avoiding it.

Having said this, we should now look at how anachronism can affect a number of different types of history. After all, it is easier to see the problems by examining a historian in action than it is by simply engaging in abstract reflection.

Anachronism and the History of Ideas

Perhaps there is no branch of history where anachronism has done more damage than the history of ideas. This is probably why the history of ideas has, indeed, been a much-maligned area. For some, ideas are of interest only as idioms by which struggles for power are expressed or masked. The ideas in themselves are thus mere accidental properties of real history and therefore unworthy of serious attention in themselves. A historian such as Sir Lewis Namier might well fall into this category. For others, ideas do represent ideological expressions of, say, class interests, and thus are worthy objects of study, but only as they serve deeper, material analysis. We looked at Christopher Hill as a representative Marxist in the last chapter, and his approach would fall into this broad category. Yet one further traditional stream of objections to the discipline is that, too often, it has not been historical enough: ideas are abstracted from their historical contexts; later criteria, which were inapplicable at the time the ideas developed, are used to judge their coherence; meanings and significance are read back into earlier ideas, texts, and philosophies, which were not really there at the time; and, as is sometimes the case particularly in fields such as the history of philosophy, political thought, and theology, the history of ideas is a surreptitious way of doing philosophy, political thought, or theology in the present, without having to engage some of the more pressing contemporary questions. Pick up any book on theology, for example, and one is likely to find statements from Augustine, John Calvin, and Karl Barth juxtaposed on the same page and brought into direct dialogue with each other; yet Augustine is separated from Calvin by over a millennium and from Barth by a millennium and a half; and that is just the time difference, without reference to geography, culture, etc. To make such connections directly looks sloppy and implies that the writer believes that ideas can easily and cleanly be abstracted from his original context.

This last type of objection is, in essence, the accusation that the history of ideas is too often driven by forms of anachronism. To abstract ideas from their historical context is to place them outside or above history; to use later standards of judgment is obviously problematic, as is reading into texts later meanings and significance; and to surreptitiously do modern philosophy via history is surely to sidestep critical questions of historical method. Yet much that goes on in the name of the history of ideas continues to be vulnerable to precisely these kinds of criticisms.

To avoid this kind of problem, the historian of ideas must first of all do something that, on the surface perhaps, appears to contradict the very task of the history of ideas: she must refuse to privilege ideas as a peculiar category of historical action. That may sound a little strange. Is the historian of ideas not one who by her stated objective is going to privilege ideas? Of course that is the case; but my point here is not that the historian should not focus on ideas, but rather that she should not regard ideas as a peculiarly ahistorical category of action. Historical actions are intentional actions performed by conscious human agents at some point in the past. That means that wars are historical actions; that empires are historical actions; that economies are historical actions; that court cases, wills, and marriages are historical actions; and that sentences, speeches, books—all of the manifestations of *ideas*—are historical actions as well, performed by historical agents. An idea has to be thought by a historical agent at a particular point in time with the intention of achieving one or more particular ends. For the idea to be understood, then, it must be subjected to the standard procedure for understanding any historical action: the diachronic and synchronic contexts must be explored in order for the intention to be elucidated. In other words, we need to establish the background to the idea in terms of the past history to which it relates (the diachronic context) and the immediate context in which it is performed (the synchronic context).

Before we look at some specific examples, it is worth reflecting for a moment on the limits of what can be done in this context. When I use the term "intention," I am specifically referring to that purpose that the author of an idea has when she expresses the idea. Two things are worth noting here.

First, and perhaps obviously, intentions are not necessarily single: in writing a book, I might well be intending to contribute to an ongoing debate, to refute a particular opponent, to introduce others to great ideas or philosophies or history, to boost my royalties to help pay for my children's education, to strengthen my case for tenure, etc. All of these intentions, and more, can co-exist with each other; all are quite possibly publicly accessible if the book is set in context and/or I care to reveal them to you; and all may well shape the way I write the book, the form of the argument, etc. In other words, an emphasis upon ideas as intentional actions by human agents does not require that I reduce intention to a single point, nor does it legitimate a simplification of human thought and action in a manner that would then facilitate simplistic historical analysis.

Some discrimination is necessary here. I could write a book on Indian cookery for Westerners, and I might say in the foreword that I wrote the book for two reasons: to introduce Westerners in general to Indian cookery, and to help my wife learn to cook Indian food properly. The first intention would be relatively easy to verify, simply by analyzing the internal contents of the book and setting the book itself within the wider context of the literary genre of cookbooks, both publicly accessible. The latter—the assertion about my wife's cooking skills—could only be verified by someone who has firsthand experience of my wife's cookery or access to other related evidence that would allow the formation of a judgment about my claim, such as a private letter or e-mail to my wife, indicating that this was why I was writing the book. Therefore, within the sphere of publicly recoverable intentions, there is a need for the historian to have an awareness of the status and basis of historical claims about these intentions and thus to be conscious of their relative provisionality. Some are easily verifiable; others less so. As always, the historian needs to be aware of the limits of evidence and to be appropriately modest in the claims to certainty that he makes.

Second, and following from this last observation, authorial intention may prove to be complex, but it is restricted to that which is recoverable from public action; as a result, it is still thus limited and always somewhat provisional. For example, I might write a book on how the early lyrics of Led Zeppelin speak to issues in analytic philosophy that were emerging in British universities in the late 1960s. This may be a bizarre and utterly wrongheaded thesis, but if the book was clearly about Zeppelin and philosophy, and was, indeed, part of a series of other books I had written, with titles such as *The Kinks and Existentialism*, *Cream and Logical Positivism*, and *The Influence of Plotinus on The Yardbirds*, then you could reasonably surmise that my intention in the Zeppelin book was to continue my project of demonstrating the relationship between classic British rock music and philosophy.

In fact, however, I might also have written the book because an early schoolmaster who bullied me in class and whom I detested happened to hate rock music and considered it to have no relation to philosophy whatsoever; given this, my writing of the series of volumes on rock and philosophy was motivated to a significant degree by my desire to take a form of belated revenge upon him. By connecting his beloved subject to a series of great rock bands, I was really wanting to inflict mental agony on this former master. Now, this reason for writing is inaccessible to you, the reader, unless I care to reveal it. Thus, I would argue that you can indeed partially reconstruct my reasons for writing—you can know my *intentions*, a term I would like to restrict to that which is publicly accessible—but you cannot exhaustively know all that is going on behind the scenes—you cannot know my *motivations*, a term I would like to restrict to that which is hidden and private, except to the extent that I choose to reveal them to you. Indeed, given the unconscious level at which the motivations for many of our actions take place, I may not know them all myself: even in the example given, I might be unaware that it is my resentment of an old teacher that drives me down such a fruitful avenue of academic study.

One further point must be made at this juncture: in saying this, I do not wish to fall prey to the so-called *intentional fallacy*, which sees the original intention of the agent or author as determining the meaning and significance of an action. I certainly want to maintain that the original intention is an important part of understanding the significance of any action; but we should avoid reducing the historical significance of any action to original intention, or restricting the kind of questions that we ask, to matters of intention. Take, for example, the letter of Pliny we discussed in the last chapter: I argued that Pliny probably reveals to us the underlying reason for the particular persecution of Christians in Pontus/ Bithynia at that time (economic hardship caused by the desertion of the local pagan temple); but I do not believe he *intended* to convey that piece of information. Rather, his naïve recounting of events revealed information that allows me as a historian to draw tentative conclusions about the background to the persecution, of the significance of which he himself may have been blissfully unaware. Thus, all that is being said here about intention is specifically related to narrow questions about the intended meaning or significance of ideas; it is not related to any attempt to reduce the meaning and significance of a particular text or idea simply to the original intention of the agent.

Given these qualifications, we can now look at a couple of examples to see how careful attention to authorial intention, recovered through careful attention to context, can help us avoid some of the more egregious results of past attempts at the history of ideas.

Example One: Comparing John Calvin and Francis Turretin

The areas of politics, philosophy, and theology have proved particularly fertile soil for historians of ideas, a point which is hardly surprising given that the stock in trade of these different disciplines is, of course, ideas. As I am most familiar with the history of theology, I will take the first example from this field, one which relates to the much debated question of how the Protestantism of the early sixteenth century relates to that of the later seventeenth century.

One very easy way of accessing this problem is to look at the work of two men, John Calvin (sixteenth century) and Francis Turretin (seventeenth century). To take the latter first, Francis Turretin was a seventeenth-century professor of theology at the Genevan Academy. Turretin wrote a major work, translated as *The Institutes of Elenctic Theology*, which is essentially the revised and published version of his lectures on controversial (hence the archaic word *elenctic*) points of divinity. Because of the similarity in title, and also perhaps Turretin's geographical location and his job—a theologian in Geneva—this work has sometimes functioned in studies of sixteenth- and seventeenth-century theology as a point of comparison with the famous book of an earlier Genevan Protestant theologian, John Calvin's *Institutes of the Christian Religion*. Calvin had been the leader of the Reformation in Geneva from the 1540s up to the early 1560s, even helping to establish the Genevan Academy in 1559, where Turretin was later to teach.

If the two texts are simply compared in terms of their internal style and content, numerous points of similarity and difference are immediately obvious. For example, in terms of similarities, we might note that both authors cover large areas of theological discussion; both authors make significant use of biblical texts in their argumentation; and both authors spend considerable time defining their positions over against those of the Catholics and the Lutherans. Yet there are also obvious differences: for example, Turretin's work is set out in terms of repeated explicit generic questions addressing each individual theological topic, whereas such is not the case in Calvin; further, Calvin does not use the medieval theological vocabulary and distinctions, nor cite medieval sources, nor deploy philosophical categories and argumentation with the same confidence and frequency as Turretin; and Turretin's work seems unremittingly polemical, a continuous series of affirmations of orthodoxy and denials of various heterodoxies and heresies.

Given all this, it is tempting to argue that what we see in the contrasts between these two works is evidence of a development in theological discourse between the eras of Calvin and Turretin which witnesses to the increasing systematization of theology in a way that withdraws from the more exegetically grounded approach of the Reformers and retreats into a polemical, philosophical, overly logical form. In so doing, it might be argued, what we have in Turretin is a fundamentally different theology and theological temperament to what we find in Calvin.

This kind of argument has been made in numerous ways over the years. Some have seen the development between Calvin and later Reformed theology as one where there is an increasing focus on predestination, to the point where it becomes the logical axiom and organizing principle of the whole of theology. Some have seen it as a regression to an earlier, medieval way of doing theology, particularly as evidenced by the resurgence in the use of scholastic vocabulary, medieval sources, and the apparent revival of Aristotle as a metaphysical and logical authority. Others have seen the development as a move toward Enlightenment rationalism, with an increasing emphasis upon the extent of natural theology (i.e., that theology which can be derived from observing the natural world, as opposed to that which comes from special revelation, such as the Bible). All of these groups have two things in common: they fail to approach the issue in a truly historical way and, in so doing, they end up imposing anachronistic criteria on seventeenth-century thought.[1]

---

[1] For a good summary of the literature and debates surrounding the development of Reformed theology, see Richard A. Muller, *After Calvin: Studies in the Development of a Theological Tradition* (New York: Oxford University Press, 2003), chaps. 4 and 5.

In order to debunk this kind of muddle-headed thinking, we should remember at the outset the basic point I made above: books, and the ideas that they contain, are historical actions performed by historical agents. Thus, the first question to ask when we approach a historical text such as the *Institutes* of Calvin or Turretin is: what are these men *doing* when they write these texts? This question in itself requires that we reflect for a moment on a further question: how do I, as a historian, establish what they are doing when they write these texts? The answer to this is simple enough: I need to establish, first of all, the diachronic and synchronic contexts of the books in hand.

Here, of course, we need to insert a caveat: as Marc Bloch, the great French historian, wrote, context is as big as the historian cares to make it. The historian is necessarily selective in what is included in the construction of context, and this inevitably shapes how the action to be set in context will be understood. Thus, we must understand that, as contexts are limited and provisional, so are historical interpretations. In saying this, however, we are not claiming that all historical interpretations are equally valid; we are simply stating that no historical interpretation can claim to give an exhaustive account of any single action. To return to the fictional example of my book on Led Zeppelin and philosophy: if the book was the only artifact available to some historian at a later point in time, with no wider context, it would presumably be clear from its contents (unless I am an utterly hopeless communicator) that the book is a study of, well, Led Zeppelin and philosophy. If the historian later discovers that it was part of a series of such books that I had written, then she could revise her original interpretation in light of this, modifying her earlier conclusions to reference the fact that the general theme of philosophy and rock music was part of an overall agenda that I had, and that this book was not a one-of-a-kind production. In this example, the earlier account is not wrong, it is merely less comprehensive than the later. If the historian then discovered my early diaries where I lament my bullying at the hands of the schoolmaster who hated rock music, and where I resolve to dedicate my life to promulgating opinions that undermine him, the interpretation can be developed and deepened yet further. Then, if the historian is also able to establish that the book was, say, originally intended to be twice the size but for some reason was shortened, and that this decision coincided with an economic recession when publishers were cutting costs, yet another element of context is added and still more refinement of the way the book is understood can take place. The key in each stage is for the historian to be self-aware and to make sure that she does not claim to offer any more definitive or comprehensive an interpretation of the book than that which is warranted by the state of the evidence.

So how do I go about understanding what Calvin and Turretin are doing in their respective works? That question is primarily a linguistic one: these are books, collections of words and sentences, with which I am dealing, so I need to understand what these sentences were doing in their particular time and place. The question I am asking—do the differences between the two books indicate fundamental changes in theology?—focuses my mind on the purpose and content, and thus the authorial intention behind the two books (remember: authorial intention is that which is publicly accessible from close, contextual reading of the text); and, taken together, these two points—the linguistic nature of the historical actions and the need to establish authorial intention—delimit the context for me. Put simply, I need to understand the linguistic conventions (vocabulary, form, style, etc.) that the two men are using, and why they are using them. That will be the primary focus of my construction of context.

In understanding Calvin's *Institutes*, then, numerous aspects commend themselves as part of the context necessary for discerning authorial intent. Calvin is writing a work that, both on the basis of internal and external evidence, is clearly connected to the various biblical commentaries that he also produced. A little digging in the wider context of sixteenth-century commentary as well as Calvin's own biographical background casts up the figure of Martin Bucer, a brilliant theologian and church leader but one whose biblical commentaries were marred by their long-windedness—a long-windedness that was in large part the result of endless theological dissertations inserted into the text. We know Calvin saw this fault in Bucer and wished to avoid it himself because of comments he makes in 1539 in the preface to his (Calvin's) commentary on Romans. Given all this, it seems legitimate to see at least part of Calvin's intention as being the production of an exegetical handbook to accompany the commentaries in a way that allows for more conciseness in the latter.

This does not, of course, exhaust the authorial intention of the book. The *Institutes* begins with an open letter to the King of France, calling for toleration of Protestants, and it ends with a section on civil government, arguing that Protestantism and civil society are not antithetical, and that Protestantism does not inevitably mean rebellion. It would therefore be arguable that part of the intention was an apologetic/political one; but it is also arguable that this is not of primary concern to the question we have in hand, which relates particularly to the theological content of the work.

Turning to Turretin's work, a few things can be immediately noted about its context. First, and perhaps most obviously, there is over a century dividing his book from Calvin's. In light of this, we might assume at the outset that some changes in literary form, even with works in the same genre, are to be expected; if they were both identical, then that would be unusual. Second, we therefore need to be aware of the broader developments that might well have impacted the way Turretin approached the subject: these might include, but need not be restricted to, the general intellectual environment, developments within the discourse of higher education, changes to the pastoral and polemical environment of Christianity, and even alterations in the political makeup and agenda of Geneva.

When we start to take some of these things into account, a more nuanced picture of the relationship between Calvin's *Institutes* and Turretin's *Institutes* emerges. To take the immediate context first, Turretin's work is the work of a university professor. Calvin may have been a great teacher and pastor, but he was not a university professor. Universities have established conventions that shape what goes on in the lecture theaters and what is written down in the textbooks. These conventions provide the background to Turretin in a way they cannot for Calvin. Thus, the use of explicit question and answer forms and the generic nature of how each of the questions is asked of each individual topic (What is it? Does it exist? What kind of thing is it?) reflect established university practice, which dates back to the twelfth and thirteenth centuries and remained largely undisrupted by the

Reformation and the Renaissance. That Calvin, being neither a university professor nor the author of a book designed to reflect university pedagogy, does not use such an established university form is scarcely surprising; but that Turretin, a university professor, uses such is not unusual. Indeed, what would be most strange and surprising would be his *nonuse* of such. As in so much history, it is, to use Sherlock Homes's phrase, the dog that *did not bark* that sets alarm bells ringing in the mind of the historian. The typical, the conventional, the normal requires no elaborate explanation: it is exactly what is to be expected. It is the strange, the peculiar, the unexpected, the unconventional that needs to be explicated.

In this context, the same applies to Turretin's use of Aristotle. By the seventeenth century, Aristotelianism was highly diverse and was represented by a number of different traditions that all looked back to the Aristotelian corpus as authoritative, though with many differences in interpretation. The important point to grasp, however, is that Aristotle's logic and, by and large, much of his metaphysics, was authoritative in the seventeenth century; indeed, it was not until Gottlob Frege in the nineteenth century that his logic was finally dethroned. When we understand this Aristotelian hegemony, Turretin's constant reference to him and his work is scarcely surprising. What is unusual—the dog that did not bark, if you like—is so much of the rhetoric of the earlier Reformers (including Luther and Calvin) against Aristotle's writings and thought. Does his "rehabilitation" by later Protestants not therefore represent a fundamental deviation from or even repudiation of earlier Protestantism?

The short answer is, no. When we look at early Protestant rejection of Aristotle, it becomes clear that it was not as comprehensive and categorical as has sometimes been claimed, but was generally targeted at specific appropriations of Aristotle by medieval theology which men such as Luther and Calvin saw as leading to a perversion of Christian teaching. Specifically, Luther saw medieval teaching on justification as being the result of an uncritical appropriation of Aristotelian definitions of righteousness: that the righteous person is the one who acts righteously. In many other areas, however, the Aristotelian corpus continued, even for Luther, to hold a high place as a basic source and authority. Indeed, it could not be otherwise, given that the comprehensive nature of the various Aristotelian worldviews meant that Aristotle's dominant role in intellectual culture could scarcely be overthrown until something equally comprehensive was found to replace it; and that only became possible with the Enlightenment.

A related issue is the resurgence in the writings of men such as Turretin of the positive use of medieval theologians and their conceptual vocabulary. Does this not represent a regression to an earlier theology that the Reformers such as Calvin repudiated? Again, the short answer is that no, this is not a necessary conclusion. Two factors need to be taken into account. First, as noted above, Turretin is working in a university context. Medieval theologians had developed an elaborate vocabulary for teaching theology in a university setting, and men such as Turretin can scarcely be blamed for not wishing to reinvent the wheel at this point. The establishment of Protestant theology within the university context involved the adopting of many of the forms of university discourse, of which medieval conceptual vocabulary was one.

Second, the elaboration and expansion of polemics in the late sixteenth and early seventeenth century and the rise of new movements such as Arminianism (a form of Reformed Protestantism that rejected predestination in favor of a view of salvation in which human decision was decisive) and Socinianism (an antimetaphysical movement that rejected the doctrines of the Trinity, incarnation, and atonement) further challenged the established orthodoxies of Catholicism and Protestantism and meant inevitably that theology required elaboration if it was to be defended. Many of the terms and arguments developed in the Middle Ages were remarkably useful for such a task. For example, the discussions of human free will and divine foreknowledge of the later medieval period were remarkably useful to Reformed Protestants in helping to defend anti-Pelagian understandings of grace over against the assaults of Arminians and Socinians. In this context, the appropriation of the conceptual vocabulary of an earlier generation is neither surprising, sinister, nor necessarily doctrinally significant in terms of marking points of deviation from the Reformers. Indeed, one might even provocatively suggest that the Reformers themselves might occasionally have benefited from a more accurate understanding of medieval theology.[2]

This is, of course, all broad context that allows us to understand some of the obvious differences between Calvin and Turretin in ways that do not require us to speculate about theological motives. These differences in form and vocabulary are all explicable in terms of the differing public context of the two men. But we can go further by adding Turretin's own stated intention: to cover the heads of disputed divinity in a way that his students, many of whom are bound for the ministry, will find useful when defending Reformed Protestantism against its opponents.[3] Now, as with all stated intentions, we should ask whether the writer speaks truth or not. In this case, the content of his *Institutes* certainly seems to be consistent with his stated intention: the book offers a reasonably comprehensive study of heads of doctrine, addressed specifically in terms of challenges to the Reformed Orthodox on each point as posed by the Catholics, the Lutherans, the Arminians, the Socinians and, on occasion, the Amyraldians (a Protestant theological party associated with the theological school at Saumur in France); and it is also consistent with what appears to be the original context for the delivery of the material that has come to be included in the book, the classroom at the Genevan Academy. Using the distinction we noted earlier, between authorial *intention* (that which is publicly recoverable) and *motivation* (that which is private and publicly inaccessible), we are not required to say that Turretin's stated purpose in writing the book exhausts all that he desired to accomplish (perhaps he was unhappily married and writing the tome gave him an excuse to stay in his

---

[2]David C. Steinmetz has argued convincingly that while Calvin explicitly rejected the standard medieval distinction between God's absolute and ordained power, he actually accepted its conceptual content. The implication is that Calvin simply did not understand what the medieval terminology was intended to convey: see David C. Steinmetz, *Calvin in Context* (New York: Oxford University Press, 1995), 40–52.

[3]"Let no one think that a full and accurate system of theology is delivered here. For this was not indeed the design proposed to me, but only to explain the importance of the principal controversies which lie between us and our adversaries (ancient and modern) and supply to the young the thread of Ariadne, by the help of which they may more easily extricate themselves from their labyrinth." From "Turretin's Preface to the Reader," *Institutes of Elenctic Theology*, trans. George Musgrave Giger, ed. James T. Dennison Jr., 3 vols. (Phillipsburg, NJ: P&R, 1992), I:xl.

study and avoid his wife!), but it does seem to offer a plausible account of why he wrote what he did. In other words, Turretin's book has a different intention to that of Calvin; indeed, given its context and purpose, it is of an entirely different genre to that of Calvin.

Once we have done this kind of work with the two texts and set them both in their respective contexts by asking questions about genre, intention, and the established conventions of the day within which the authors worked, we are in a position to see how inadequate is any attempt to compare and contrast the two works by simply looking at the two texts in isolation. Our interest may well be in the question of whether the theology of the two men is different, but we cannot begin to answer that question simply by the use of theological or doctrinal categories abstracted from historical context. The contextual work needs to be done first. These books are historical actions and need to be understood historically before we can start addressing any such questions about differences in content in any thoughtful way.

One last point here is the possible objection that, in doing this work, I have erased all the differences between Calvin and Turretin and argued that the difference between the two is one of form, not content; and, as anyone who has read any literary theory will know, you cannot cleanly separate form and content any more than you can cleanly separate text from context. Can we not posit fundamental differences between Calvin and Turretin on the grounds of fundamental differences in form? Now, I am not naïve enough to believe that there can be a simple separation of form and content, but it is one thing to say that form and content cannot be neatly separated and quite another thing to say that this particular form requires this particular content, or vice versa. Turretin's work operates very clearly within a form of discourse, both in terms of overall structure and much of its technical vocabulary, which dates back to the twelfth century; but his theology is distinctively Reformed, not medieval. The presence of the medieval form does not require or presuppose medieval content. Indeed, medieval scholasticism itself enjoyed a basic common form and vocabulary, but was highly diverse, as a comparison of Thomas Aquinas with John Duns Scotus or William of Occam will quickly corroborate. My point relative to Calvin and Turretin, therefore, is not here to argue that they hold to the same basic theology expressed in two different forms, though that may be substantially the case; it is rather that arguments based simply on the respective forms of the two works are not sufficient in themselves to establish either the internal contents of their thought or the points of fundamental differences between their two theologies. That work must be done by, among other things, a careful attention to both the wider context and the internal content of their respective works.

Example Two: Was Luther a Racist?

If the first example we looked at provides an example of anachronism in terms of abstracting texts from context, this second example provides an example of how later categories of thought or morality can be imposed on earlier eras in ways that distort our understanding of the period or the person being studied. Many times this is a somewhat tricky issue: we have already noted in chapter 1 that it is perfectly acceptable for a historian to be politically engaged, to have moral commitments, etc. Indeed, it is surely unreasonable to expect a historian to be otherwise. Nevertheless, it is one thing to have moral commitments; it is another thing to allow those commitments fundamentally to distort our understanding of why particular individuals or groups believed and acted the way they did in times past. This can be done in a number of ways, perhaps most obviously by the imposition of categories that would have been incomprehensible at an earlier point in time.

Of course, to the radical postmodernist, for whom the telling of history is about power struggles in the present rather than what happened way back when, this is not an issue. The radical feminist has no problem in highlighting the chauvinism of yesteryear, simply because her agenda is to debate women's issues in the present, even if what she dubs "chauvinism" was not understood as such at the time. The Marxist can easily spot class oppression because that is the *a priori*, idealist framework which he brings to bear, even if the whole idea of class, as conceived by a Marxist, may not actually be easy to define when it comes to former societies. And, before we thank the Lord that we are not like other men, think of slavery: how many of us find slavery obnoxious, and thus struggle to explain the commitment to it that we find in otherwise liberal figures, such as Jefferson? Is it not difficult to write about Jefferson and not feel the need to condemn him for his attitude to slaves and his relationship with Sally Hemings? How would/should we write about this topic today?

One good example of the tricky nature of such a historical task is the question of Martin Luther and the Jews. Indeed, if there is one thing everybody, whether churched or unchurched, knows about Luther, it is that he hated Jews and was partially responsible for the stream of German anti-Semitism that culminated in the Holocaust. In 1543, he wrote an infamous treatise, *On the Jews and Their Lies* in which he launched a blistering attack on the Jews, and this book has come to tar his reputation in a way that almost nothing else he wrote—with the possible exception of his attacks on the peasants in 1525—has done.

The first major problem with Luther and the Jews from a historical point of view is simply this: the Holocaust. That Luther was a German and that he wrote in such extreme ways about the Jews and what should be done to them, including systematic murder, seems to cry out for comparison with the brutality of the Nazis. Take, for example, the following passages in the work:

> First, to set fire to their synagogues or schools and to bury and cover with dirt whatever will not burn, so that no man will ever again see a stone or cinder of them.... Second, I advise that their houses also be razed and destroyed. ... Third, I advise that all their prayer books and Talmudic writings, in which such idolatry, lies, cursing, and blasphemy are taught, be taken from them.... Fourth, I advise that their rabbis be forbidden to teach henceforth on pain of loss of life and limb.... Fifth, I advise that safe-conduct on the highways be abolished completely for the Jews.[4]

---

[4]Martin Luther, "On the Jews and Their Lies" in *Christian in Society IV* (ed. Franklin Sherman; vol. 47 of *Luther's Works*, ed. Jaroslav Pelikan and Helmut T. Lehmann; Philadelphia: Fortress, 1971), 268–70.

Given the extremity of these statements and the fact that these suggestions seem to adumbrate some of the things that the Third Reich did to the Jews, some have gone as far as to suggest a causal connection between Luther and the atrocities of the 1930s and 1940s.[5] Thus, the temptation for historians approaching the topic of Luther on this issue is to do one of two things: either to make a simplistic connection between him and the Holocaust or to make every effort to acquit him of blame. In either case, the approach to Luther is being driven by issues surrounding a later event, the Holocaust, and the potential for distortion is profound.

In order to address this issue, we need to do a number of things. First, hard as it may be to do, we should set aside the Holocaust as an issue as we approach the subject. This is not to say that we should cease to have strong opinions about what happened in Germany between 1933 and 1945, or about those who have written hatefully about the Jews; but it is to say that we should not allow these things to become factors in our initial analysis of Luther's writings on the matter. The Holocaust may be part of our context, but it is part of neither the synchronic nor diachronic context of Luther's original work; it had no impact on his historical action at this point. Second, as we set aside such later concerns, so we should at the same time set about establishing what the conventions were in Luther's day for talking about the Jews. Once we know the background against which Luther was working, we can see in what ways his writing was typical or atypical of his day.

This second point falls into two related parts. First, we need to see what kind of writing was typical at the time: Was it usual to be anti-Jewish? What sort of things did anti-Jewish writers say? Were there various stock-in-trade criticisms of the Jews that occur again and again in sixteenth-century works? This will allow us to make an assessment of how exceptional Luther's sentiments and arguments were, and thus to discern what, if any, distinctive contribution to the history of anti-Jewish polemic he made. As noted earlier, in history it is the exceptional things, not the ordinary, that

---

[5]See William L. Shirer, *The Rise and Fall of the Third Reich* (London: Secker and Warburg, 1960), 91.

require explanation; but one can only discern the exceptional once one knows what "ordinary" is in a given context.

Second, we need also to establish what kinds of categories were used in thinking about the Jews. It is very clear, for example, that Nazi actions regarding the Jews were framed in racial categories, and that the differences between Jews and others were therefore seen in biological, racial terms. Even if such categories were ultimately built on pseudoscience, that does not make the racial category any less significant in understanding the mindset and the intentions of Nazi Germany. But was it the case that Luther and his contemporaries used racial categories, or did they see the issue with Jews in terms of other factors?

If we stop for a moment's reflection at this point, we can already see the direction in which our analysis will take us. By approaching the topic in this way, we avoid making the Holocaust and Nazi Germany the dominant criteria by which to assess Luther's actions; instead, we determine at the outset to understand why he wrote what he did about the Jews at the time at which he did so. In other words, we are seeking to explain his action in historical terms and not to make moral criteria a foundational part of our historical method.

On the first point, contemporary writing on the Jews, even a cursory glance at literature on Judaism in the sixteenth century reveals that anti-Jewish polemic was not invented by Luther but had a longstanding and well-established pedigree, stretching back into the Middle Ages and beyond. Indeed, literary attacks on Jews and Judaism can be found back as far as the end of the first century and beginning of the second, as the two religions, Christianity and Judaism, parted ways. The late second-century account, *The Martyrdom of Polycarp*, for example, contains gratuitous references to the involvement of Jews in Polycarp's public execution. Later, Ambrose, fourth-century bishop of Milan, defended the soldier Kynegius who had conducted a campaign of synagogue burning in the East. As to the Middle Ages, Jews had been violently persecuted in Europe for several centuries before Luther arrived on the scene. For example, they were expelled from England in 1290 by Edward I. This was only one of the more extreme examples of judicial persecution and it was certainly not unique. Even worse were the events in Spain in 1391, when up to a third of the Jewish population was massacred and a third forcibly converted to Christianity. Being a Jew in European Christendom was difficult and dangerous.

Of course, such things do not happen in a vacuum, and we can see in literature from the twelfth century onward that lurid tales of Jewish atrocities against Christians were a common part of European culture. The so-called "blood libel" was particularly popular and widespread. This was the claim that Jews kidnapped Christian children and offered them in ritual sacrifice, and it is clearly part of a culture that treated Jews with deep suspicion and fear. In such contexts, stories such as the blood libel could serve to exacerbate hatred and lead to persecution, such as that which occurred in Lincoln in 1255 when a little child was kidnapped and murdered, and a Jew named Copin confessed that it was the practice of Jews to kidnap and crucify a child each year. Such tales became standard parts of the anti-Jewish culture of medieval Europe.

In addition to all of this unequivocally anti-Jewish background, even some actions that, on the surface, might appear to indicate the existence of a strong pro-Jewish counterculture in the sixteenth century, turn out on closer inspection to be far different. The so-called Reuchlin Affair is a case in point. In 1509 a converted Jew, Johannes Pfefferkorn, argued that all extrabiblical Jewish literature should be destroyed, and was opposed by one of the leading humanist scholars of his day, Johannes Reuchlin. It might be tempting to see this as a straightforward battle between some-one who in today's parlance would be described as a self-hating Jew and a philo-Semite. But was that really the case? Pfefferkorn had earlier argued against the notion of the blood libel and had thus tried to defend the Jews against the typical kinds of slander and subsequent persecution that they so often had to endure. In fact, as has been demonstrated by historian Heiko Oberman, Pfefferkorn's position is far more complicated than a question of self-hating Jew versus scholar: Pfefferkorn's intention in wanting Jewish literature destroyed appears to have been to prevent what he regarded as false biblical interpretation from being spread abroad; Reuchlin, whatever his private scholarly motivations might have been, certainly made the public case that preserving this literature allowed people to see just how twisted the Jews were—hardly an obvious case of philo-Semitism.[6]

Given the widespread nature of anti-Jewish literature and sentiment from the late Middle Ages, the fact that Luther wrote against the Jews starts to look less like an exceptional occurrence and more typical of its age. Anti-Judaism in western European Christendom is the norm in Luther's time and thus *On the Jews and Their Lies* stands within an established, dominant tradition of Christian writings on Jews. Indeed, given the fact that he even makes use of the blood libel, we can clearly see just how conventional the work is. For example:

> I have read and heard many stories about the Jews which agree with this judgment of Christ, namely, how they have poisoned wells, made assassinations, kidnapped children, as related before.[7]

Luther is here self-consciously positioning himself within an established tradition of anti-Jewish writings upon which he draws.

In light of this, we might decide to stop at this point and say, OK, it is clear that Luther actually contributes little or anything that is original to writings on the Jews in the sixteenth century; even he indicates the conventional nature of his claims. However, as I said earlier, it is only once one has established what is normal, routine, and conventional that one can then discern what is unusual and unexpected; and, as it happens, Luther did write a strange treatise on the Jews— it just happens not to be the one of which most people are aware.

What is really unusual about Luther's writings on the Jews is not the violent outburst of hate against them in 1543, but rather his earlier work of 1523, *That Jesus Was Born a Jew*, which is surprisingly positive about the Jews.[8] This raises the interesting question of why Luther changed his

---

[6]See Heiko A. Oberman, *The Roots of Anti-Semitism in the Age of Renaissance and Reformation* (Philadelphia: Fortress Press, 1984).

[7]Martin Luther, "On the Jews and Their Lies," 47:277; cf. 217, 264, 267.

[8]See, for example, the concluding paragraph: "If we really want to help them, we must be guided in our dealings with them not by papal law but by the law of Christian love. We must receive them cordially, and permit them to trade and work with us, that they may have occasion and opportunity to associate with us, hear our Christian teaching, and witness our Christian life. If some of them should prove

mind, the answer to which is actually very germane to the whole issue of Luther and the Jews, yet which could not even be appropriately addressed unless one realized that it was the treatise of 1523, not 1543, which was exceptional by the conventional standards of the day.

Before we can address this question of why Luther was able to write positively about the Jews earlier in his career, we need to spend a few moments reflecting on the question, why are the Jews so hated? We can be helped in this by drawing contrasts between the Reformation era and the Nazi regime in the twentieth century. The answer in Germany during the Third Reich is very simple: Jews are an inferior race and must be exterminated as vermin. Such is very clear from the Nuremberg Laws of 1935. These laws restricted German citizenship to "a national of German or kindred blood," defined Jews as not being of German blood, and forbade all marriages between Jews and German nationals and all extramarital sexual relations between Jews and Germans.[9] Thus, the concepts underlying the very legal basis of what then took place, culminating in the death camps, was biological not religious. A Jew who converted to Christianity was still going to be a Jew, because conversion did not provide him or her with the relevant blood type.

The conceptual basis for Nazi anti-Semitism is thus racial, based on biology. Now, the fact that the biology underlying Nazi ideology is spurious may well be significant in refuting Nazism, but it is not significant in understanding how the Third Reich thought and acted. After all, it should be obvious that a belief does not have to be true in order to impact motives and intentions, to shape social behavior or policy, and to provide an explanation for action. For example, I might be absolutely convinced that I can fly to the moon under my own steam, and, under this delusion, I might jump off the top of the Empire State Building: my belief will not carry me to the moon, but neither will knowledge of the laws of gravity

---

stiff-necked, what of it? After all, we ourselves are not all good Christians either." Martin Luther, "That Jesus Was Born a Jew" in *Christian in Society II* (ed. Walther I. Brandt; vol. 45 of *Luther's Works*, ed. Jaroslav Pelikan and Helmut T. Lehmann; Philadelphia: Fortress, 1962), 229.

[9] Martin Gilbert, *The Holocaust: A History of the Jews of Europe during the Second World War* (New York: Holt, 1985), 47–48.

allow others to understand my intention in jumping, though it may allow them to assess me as being completely mad.

This is where the world of Luther and the world of the Third Reich are so different. For Luther, the problem with Jews is a fundamentally religious one, as it was for all western European societies during the late Middle Ages. Luther had no real concept of race in the way that we do today. His world was one of religious categories, not biological or pseudo-biological ones. For him the problem was thus one of ideological commitment, connected to the issue of social assimilation. To put it bluntly: how does a society where the state and the church are essentially two sides of the same coin assimilate those who, by their very definition, are not members of the latter? The answer is simple: either it does not assimilate them and instead persecutes them, or it tries to convert them (either by persuasion or by force) and thus make them part of the church. Once converted, the problem ceases because it is an issue of religious conviction, not one of race. A Jew who becomes a Christian is easy to fit into a society, all good members of which are baptized and respect the church.

This, in fact, allows us to explain what I have already noted as the most perplexing thing about Luther's approach to the Jews: his dramatic change of mind. The reason for the gentle and somewhat exceptional attitude to the Jews in the 1523 treatise is religious. Luther thinks that the Reformation will carry all before it; and, like many Christian before and since, he thinks he is living at the end of time where the return of Christ will be heralded by a mass conversion of the Jews. Indeed, there can be no doubt that Luther desired to see the Jews converted to Christianity because he was convinced that he was living at the end of time when the eschatological conversion was imminent. Thus, near the end of the treatise he expresses himself as follows:

> If the Jews should take offense because we confess our Jesus to be a man, and yet true God, we will deal forcefully with that from Scripture in due time. But this is too harsh for a beginning. Let them first be suckled with milk, and begin by recognizing this man Jesus as the true Messiah; after that they may drink wine, and learn also that he is true God. For they have been

led astray so long and so far that one must deal gently with them, as people who have been all too strongly indoctrinated to believe that God cannot be man. Therefore, I would request and advise that one deal gently with them and instruct them from Scripture; then some of them may come along. Instead of this we are trying only to drive them by force, slandering them, accusing them of having Christian blood if they don't stink, and I know not what other foolishness. So long as we thus treat them like dogs, how can we expect to work any good among them? Again, when we forbid them to labor and do business and have any human fellowship with us, thereby forcing them into usury, how is that supposed to do them any good?[10]

The purpose of the treatise is apologetic and evangelistic, advocating behavior that will serve to bring the Jews into the Christian fold. By the time Luther writes his polemic against the Jews in 1543, it is clear that the expected mass conversion will not be taking place, at least in his lifetime, and thus he reverts to the more typical idiom of Jew baiting, albeit in an extreme form, even by the exacting standards of the time. This, it would seem to me, is a plausible account of the change.

Given all this, how do we then approach the connection between Luther and the Holocaust? First, it is plain that any straightforward causal connection is inappropriate: four centuries separate the two things, and it is also clear that Luther was far from unique in articulating anti-Jewish sentiment in the late Middle Ages. He was neither the founder, nor the sole example of it in his day and generation.

Second, we need to understand that to use the Holocaust as a grid through which to read Luther's writings on the Jews is anachronistic on at least two levels. It runs the risk of seeing Luther as an exceptional figure, in terms of both writing and influence, and it fails to see that the categories with which Luther thinks about the issue (religious) are not those with which, say, Hitler thought about the issue (racial).

All this is not to say that the historian today needs to approve of what Luther said or to excuse it; but it is to demand that the historian understand the significance of Luther's historical action in terms of the categories and

---

[10]Martin Luther, "That Jesus Was Born a Jew," 45:229.

issues of his day, not those of the mid-twentieth century. Does this mean we should see no relationship between Luther and the Holocaust? By no means. But that question needs to be answered in a manner that takes into account all that has been said thus far. In fact, I would suggest two possible ways that we might address the issue, neither of which are vulnerable to the kind of anachronistic fallacy outlined above.

First, we could look at the historical evidence to see whether Luther's writings on the Jews are part of an ongoing tradition of anti-Jewish writing in European culture that stretches back to the Middle Ages and forward to the Holocaust. Certainly, the use of things such as the blood libel and the persistence of such myths throughout the centuries would suggest that such might be a very fruitful study, and one that would not exclude clear acknowledgment of the changing categories that anti-Jewish literature utilizes. This kind of study does not require us to posit naïve causal connections between the sixteenth and the twentieth century, nor to deny significant differences between the two eras; but it does allow us to understand how anti-Jewish feeling was expressed, how it functioned within European society over a protracted period of time, and how both Luther and the Holocaust fit into this narrative.

Second, we could study the reception of Luther's writings in later anti-Semitic writing and how his book was actually used by those involved in the ideological construction and defense of the policies of the Third Reich. In this way, we are really looking not at what Luther *said* so much as *how he was used by later anti-Semites*. Indeed, his status as a German-speaker and as a hater of the Jews inevitably enhanced his usefulness to the Nazis. What we must not do, however, is confuse this reception of Luther in Nazi writings and propaganda with his original intention, which is effectively what William Shirer did. To do that would be to fall back into anachronism.[11]

---

[11]Luther continues to be a useful source for anti-Semites: see http://www.biblebelievers.org.au/luther. htm/, where *On the Jews and Their Lies* is excerpted on a Web site that elsewhere refers to Auschwitz as a "'ten-star hotel'...'where Jews were sent for their own protection,'" http://biblebelievers.org.au/nl506.htm (accessed October 27, 2008).

Conclusion

The two examples of anachronism above should make it clear both what the problems are and how one can approach historical issues in a way that, while not requiring one to do the impossible and disengage from present commitments, at least facilitates an approach to historical questions that attempts to place the historical intentions of the authors of various actions at the center of analysis, and not the agendas, concerns, or categories of later eras.

In both examples, the vital importance of understanding the conventions of the day is obvious. With Calvin, it is important to understand how he relates to the established commentary tradition and the developing use of commonplace books and rhetoric in order to understand what it is pedagogically that he is attempting to do in his *Institutes*. For Turretin, a knowledge of the nature of university education, of the increasingly complex polemical context, and of the importance of medieval and Aristotelian concepts and vocabulary is crucial to grasping what he is intending to do in his book. A comparison between the two books, therefore, that simply engages in point-by-point comparison of the style, structure, and overall aesthetics is really a pointless exercise from a historical perspective. The books look different. So what? To leap to judgments about the transformation of theology in the century that separates them is a giant leap indeed, and certainly unwarranted until the heavy lifting of setting the works in context has been done.

With Luther, we need to avoid the tendency to see his revolting anti-Jewish rhetoric of 1543 as exceptional, for then we will be tempted to make his treatise more significant than it was. By studying the established traditions and conventions of anti-Jewish works we can see that it is exceptional only in its extremity; and that, in fact, much of the sentiment is extremely conventional and merely part of a much wider tradition. Only then can we also see that it is really his 1523 treatise that is exceptional, and that the interesting question regarding Luther and the Jews is not why did he write so hatefully about them, but why did he change his mind? In asking that question, we open up whole new vistas of exploration of Luther's self-understanding that might otherwise have been closed to us, or at least more obscure.

In approaching historical actions, then, historians have a hard task in front of them. They need to do more than just look at the war or the book or the speech that is of interest to them in particular; they need to look at the relevant conventions that shaped the human behavior of the time during which the specific historical action to be studied occurred. Only once the conventions of the day are understood can individual actions be judged aright by the standards of their day. Only then will the historian be able to judge whether a particular action is significant because it represents a defiance of or break from convention, or less significant, or even insignificant, because it is merely a replication of things said and done so often at the time that it is exactly what one would expect.

This is wide-ranging and interdisciplinary work, and indicates how important it is for historians to immerse themselves in their chosen periods of study. It also flags up the need to be self-conscious and self-critical relative to the categories which we, as historians, use. Nationalism is just one example: use it with reference to the world before the nineteenth century, and one is already utilizing a category that will produce distorted, anachronistic results.

It is also once again a reminder of the need for modesty in conclusions. Because contexts are as large as the historian cares to make them, conclusions are necessarily limited and provisional. Again, this is not to say that all conclusions are therefore equally valid, that all histories are equally true; but it is to say that no history can lay claim to enjoying a status that means it can never be improved or refined as a result of fresh discoveries or insights.

Finally, to make a specific comment on my own discipline, that of intellectual history, many of the problems that are associated with this can be defused once it is acknowledged that ideas enjoy no privileged status in comparison with other historical actions. On the contrary, by thinking of ideas as actions, the appropriate way of approaching them as historians is surely made a lot clearer: context is crucial to meaning.

CHAPTER 4

A Fistful of Fallacies

In this final chapter, I want to offer a brief survey of some of the more common fallacies that historians commit. It is by no means exhaustive, and the reader who wants to read more about these kinds of issues should consult the old but still very useful, and at times very funny, book by David Hackett Fischer, *Historians' Fallacies: Toward a Logic of Historical Thought*.[1] Fischer deals with so many fallacies in such a devastatingly clear and ruthless manner that most, if not all, of us will blush as we read it, recognizing our own foolishness and ineptitude at various points in his narrative.

This chapter, by contrast, is a much more modest affair, focusing on just a fistful of classic errors in the hope that even this small selection will provoke some remedial embarrassment in enough readers to have made the effort worthwhile.

---

[1]David Hackett Fischer, *Historians' Fallacies: Toward a Logic of Historical Thought* (New York: Harper & Row, 1970).

Reification

One of the constant refrains throughout this book has been that history is an interpretative exercise. It depends upon the identification and selection of what constitutes evidence and the organization of that evidence into a narrative that tells a certain tale about the past. In the chapter on explanatory schemes, I made the point that this involves the historian bringing to bear on the past certain interpretative models or grids that allow for the task to be executed. I also indicated that the ever-present danger in such schemes is that their descriptive intention is hard to separate from their prescriptive impact; indeed, they can easily become prescriptive in a manner that prevents their own falsifiability.

Closely related to this is the problem of reification. According to Webster's dictionary, *reification* is "the process or result of reifying," and *reifying* is "to regard (something abstract) as a material or concrete thing." In other words, reification is the act by which an abstraction is given an existence it does not really possess and, from the historian's perspective, can therefore take on a life of its own. It ceases to be the endterm of a process of historical interpretation and becomes rather something that stands as an *a priori* category of analysis.

Before looking at the problems such reifications might cause, it is worth citing a few examples in order to highlight what exactly is meant. Take the term "socialism," for example. Most people would agree that there are—or at least there were until recently—socialists in the world. The term was used to describe people who were committed to certain approaches to social and economic issues and organization. Used in this way, the term is helpful in distinguishing certain individuals or groups and locating them on the political spectrum. Yet there is a sense in which "socialism" as such does not exist in the way that, say, the British Labour Party exists. The Labour Party has a material existence: it has a constitution; it owns property; it has a membership list; it has legal status; as an institution, it has performed certain actions over the years, such as holding conferences, fighting elections, passing legislation, nationalizing industries, denationalizing industries, etc. Socialism, by contrast, has no such material or institutional existence.

Further, it is hard to argue that all those typically called "socialists" enjoy universal agreement on any particular idea or a body of ideas: for example, both communists and social democrats have been typically embraced by the term in various histories. Instead, it is rather an abstraction that can be used to connect, say, the policies of the Labour Party with analogous movements and parties elsewhere in both time and space. As such it is very useful in that it brings out what we might call family resemblances between such movements and institutions; but we need to be aware that it is limited precisely because it is an abstraction and not something tied to a specific institution or building or self-identifying group of people in a single organization.

A second example might be "theological liberalism" as used with reference to theology. Again, unlike, say, Anglicanism, this term has little or no specific concrete existence. It is not the monopoly of any particular institution or church; rather it is a term that is variously applied to a variety of different theologies. Because in some contexts it is seen as pejorative, it is also a term that has a rather elastic meaning: for historians of doctrine, it is used very precisely to refer to the theological response to the critical philosophy of Immanuel Kant, as epitomized in the work of men such as F. D. E. Schleiermacher or Albrecht Ritschl. To the Primitive Baptist in the South of the United States of America, it might refer to anybody who professes Christian faith but drinks alcohol or uses a Bible translation other than the King James Version. Any relationship between the two usages is highly tenuous.

This second example actually leads us to the problem that reification poses for the historian: as helpful as such terms are for identifying, organizing, and interpreting data historically, they can take on an independent existence and become less descriptive and more prescriptive of the historical task. Once the term "liberalism" takes on a life of its own, then connections that may not exist in reality are given a kind of existence. Thus, there is no real connection between the work of Schleiermacher and my own liking for an occasional glass of beer or wine after a hard day's work; but if both are examples of "liberalism," then the illusion is created of a real connection between the two phenomena. Denial of the resurrection and drinking a glass of homebrew become part and parcel of a larger ideal of "liberalism" and thus can be connected in ways that, frankly, they should not be. The phenomena of history become subordinate to an abstraction that now functions as a prescriptive tool.

A good example of reification that has impacted in unfortunate ways the writing of history is that of Aristotelianism. As is well known, Aristotle was the greatest pupil of the philosopher Plato, and he offered a way of understanding reality that differed in significant ways from that of his teacher. In a series of elaborate logical, scientific, and metaphysical texts, he offered the world a fairly comprehensive understanding of reality, such that his philosophical corpus became the dominant resource for thought both in the Latin West and, interestingly enough, in the Arabic East, for nearly two millennia after his death. Indeed, his physics was only dethroned by the work of such as Isaac Newton (seventeenth century), his metaphysics by such as David Hume and Immanuel Kant (eighteenth century), and his logic by Gottlob Frege (nineteenth century).

The story of the transmission and reception of Aristotle in the West is interesting. The sixth-century Christian philosopher, Boethius, had desired to translate all of Aristotle into Latin, but death by execution intervened before he could move beyond the *Organon*, or logical treatises. Then, it was not until the twelfth century that Latin translations of Arabic translations became available in the West, causing something of an intellectual crisis for the church, which had hitherto accepted Aristotle's authority as a logician and was now faced with the fact that he did not seem too sound on issues such as the creation of the world. This is where Albert the Great and his even greater pupil, Thomas Aquinas, became significant. Indeed, in the life and work of Aquinas, the church found the man who was able to appropriate Aristotle for the Christian faith in a manner that did not involve the abandonment of orthodoxy.

While Aquinas was without doubt the single most important and influential example of the reception of Aristotle in Western intellectual history, it is worth noting that his reception was via translations and was not the only possible approach to the philosopher's work. His agenda was to appropriate Aristotle in a manner that reinforced Christian orthodoxy and offered a view of the wider world that did not stand in opposition to the same. Other more radical figures, such as Siger of Brabant, used Aristotle for more dramatic agendas. Then during the Reformation, a time when the Greek language became once again a commonplace for scholars, Philip Melanchthon had a polemically-driven vision to produce a new edition of Aristotle that would effectively repristinate his thought and allow others to judge how well or badly he had been used by Catholic theologians.

All of this is to say that the reception of Aristotle's thought is so varied and complex that the term "Aristotelianism" does not in itself possess any unqualified content. Indeed, if the term is to be applied beyond the strict teachings of Aristotle himself, perhaps the best that can be said about the term is that it can be used to refer to thinkers or to schools of thought that look to the original Aristotelian corpus as being, in some way, authoritative or a useful resource. Such a definition is useful, but only in a very limited, highly restricted sense, and it is incumbent upon those who use the term to remember this as they employ it.

What happens if the highly qualified nature of the term is forgotten? Then Aristotelianism becomes reified, and the term comes to be understood—and indeed used—as referring to a specific set of philosophical dogmas that, rather like house bricks or buckets of paint, can be assumed to have a certain stable content and consistent impact or use that is generally independent of the specific context in which they may be found. The results can, on one level, be quite amusing; on another, they can be simply representative of bad history.

Take, for example, the argument proposed by the German theologian Ernst Bizer, British theologian T. F. Torrance, and historian Alan C. Clifford that Reformed theology after Calvin was fundamentally distorted by the appropriation of Aristotelian metaphysics in a manner that made it more causal, logical, and predestinarian.[2] There are many criticisms that can be leveled at the basic thesis offered by these writers. As many postmodern

---

[2]Ernst Bizer, *Frühorthodoxie und Rationalismus* (Zurich: EVZ-Verlag, 1963); T. F. Torrance, "One Aspect of the Biblical Conception of Faith," *Expository Times* 68 (1956–1957), 111–14; Alan C. Clifford, *Atonement and Justification: English Evangelical Theology 1640–1790: An Evaluation* (Oxford: Clarendon Press, 1990).

thinkers have correctly pointed out, it is not possible to make a clean and clear distinction between form and content, and thus the presence of Aristotelian language and forms is significant. Nevertheless, even if such clean separation is not possible, this is not the same as to argue that a particular form *necessarily* requires a particular content. Yet that seems to be what is argued here; indeed the argument represents something of a commitment to the "root fallacy"—the idea that the root of a word is determinative of its meaning and that words as such therefore carry around a certain metaphysical essence in and of themselves (itself, incidentally, a species of reification). If such was a good way of proceeding, then the popular American pastime of "football" would, presumably, require that feet were used in connection with a ball far more often than hands, something that is manifestly not the case. But, more problematic even than the apparent commitment to the root fallacy is the commitment to the idea that "Aristotelianism" can be deployed as a term without being specific about exactly what its reference is, and in a manner such that its effects are straightforward and consistent, such that the presence of "Aristotelianism" leads inevitably to the presence of certain results.

In fact, as I have argued above, "Aristotelianism" is a useful term only insofar as it points to the general dependence of Western thought on Arisotle's works, vocabulary, and the traditions that stem from the same; once it takes on a life of its own as a monolithic reification, it short-circuits the kind of careful textual analysis, empirical study, and interpretative synthesis that is found in the best historical scholarship. As such, it is a good example of the dangers inherent in this particular fallacy.

Oversimplification

One of the perennial temptations of the historian can be to oversimplify when constructing an explanation. This is what we might call one of the fallacies of causality. We have already noted this kind of problem with regard to our discussion of Marxism: Marxists are committed to a view of historical reality that sees dialectical materialism and class struggle as being of the very essence of history; and, lo and behold, their analysis confirms their convictions, while all counterevidence can be screened out or explained away on the basis of false consciousness. The resulting narratives may be articulated in very sophisticated ways and built upon very sophisticated research, but they are in fact rather simplistic in their basic assertion about the dynamic of historical movement.

The truth is that historical actions, as I have noted before, are complex because the contexts in which they occur and the agents by whom they are intended and executed are complex and stand in a complex relationship to each other. To take an example: the American Declaration of Independence is the result of trivial factors—material production (somebody made the ink and paper, both of which actions stood within a history of ink and paper production) and travel (the signers had to get from home to where they signed it)—and less trivial issues, such as a general history of political theory, the history of the Colonies, the economic struggles of the times, the political tensions in Britain, and the many individual life experiences that brought Jefferson and his colleagues to such a moment. No historian can do justice to all of these aspects. Indeed, to attempt to do so would run the risk of losing any possibility of narrative coherence, and so selectivity is crucial; but in being selective, one must acknowledge the limited nature of the story being told compared to the actual reality to which the story refers. To say that the tea tax caused the American Revolution is to speak truth, but only in the highly qualified sense that the tea tax was one part of the complex of actions that led to the Revolution.

Perhaps a more pertinent example, from a methodological perspective, of the need to be sensitive to complexity as a historian relates to the issue of literary texts. As someone primarily interested in the history of ideas, my basic sources as a historian are literary documents: books, essays, diaries, notebooks, pamphlets, published speeches, etc. Literary texts are excellent historical artifacts precisely because they can be so complicated. This is not to say that all are such: a shopping list is a shopping list; it tells you what a particular person wanted to buy at a certain point in time and thus may give fascinating insights into diet, or local economies, or even the existence of transport systems if the items could not have been produced locally. But it is likely that such a list is a fairly straightforward phenomenon.

When it comes to more complex literary productions—essays, pamphlets, speeches, biographies—it is important as a historian to be sensitive to complexity. We have already seen in our brief glance at Pliny's letter to Trajan how a writer can divulge more about his context than he himself might be aware he is doing. Pliny's casual comment that the trade in meat for sacrifice had picked up again since he had quashed the Christian sect gives the reader an important clue as to who might have been the anonymous informers. That is a good example of the need to read between the lines, as the old cliché has it.

Yet sometimes the complexity of a document can be embodied in the very intention of the author, as a careful study of the work in context can reveal. One such literary piece is the fourth-century *Life of Anthony* by Athanasius, Bishop of Alexandria, to which I referred in chapter 1.

A surface reading of the text would lead to the straightforward conclusion that Athanasius is doing simply that which he claims in the opening paragraphs: setting forth a life of the third- and fourth-century Anchorite, or desert holy man, Anthony, so that those who wish to copy the kind of piety that he exemplified may do so. Certainly, the text reads quite convincingly as such a life: it recounts Anthony's youth, his conversion to Christianity, his apprenticeship to a hermit, his various acts of self-denial and asceticism, some of his miracles, his popularity, his theology (expressed in a stylized speech), and finally his death at the staggering age of 105.

Such a simple reading, however, throws up a number of problems: first, while we know that Anthony did exist and was a desert hermit, there is little that can be done to verify many of the claims that Athanasius makes for him. Thus, its usefulness as a historical source on Anthony is limited, although the claim that Anthony was apprenticed in his way of life indicates that he was not the first to engage in such a calling, a useful point that can be verified and thus open the way to an understanding of the broad late third-century context; and the closing claim that Athanasius had received his fleece on his death was presumably something which could easily have been refuted by Athanasius's opponents (who were many and powerful) and is therefore highly likely to be true.

It is far more useful, however, to treat Athanasius's *Life of Anthony* less as just a biographical account of Anthony and more as a complex historical action in itself. In this way, it comes to serve the historian well as offering insights into the fourth-century mind. Far from being a simple biographical sketch, it becomes a means of understanding the tensions within the Christian church in the mid to late fourth century as discussions of the nature and person of the second person of the Trinity reached fever pitch in the ongoing so-called Arian controversy in the years between the Council of Nicea (325) and the Council of Constantinople (381).

In fact, a close reading of the text indicates that the *Life of Anthony* is a complex document in which Athanasius scores a large number of points, both theological and political (to the extent that the two can be separated in the world of the fourth century).

First, we already noted earlier that Anthony's crossing of the Arsenoitic Canal without being harmed by crocodiles was both a miracle story and, given the identification of such reptiles with Egyptian gods, a statement about the superiority of Christianity over pagan religion. In fact, this polemical aspect of the treatise can be extended, for the virtues of asceticism were well established in the ancient world (as with cynic philosophers such as Diogenes) as was the genre of biography designed not so much to recount with referential precision the events of a life as to create certain moral impact. In the *Life of Anthony*, what Athanasius does is make the point that Christian ascetics are superior to pagan ascetics, and he does so using the classical genre of a biography built around anecdotes which possess inspirational moral force rather than historical precision as now understood. Indeed, this superiority of Christianity to paganism is reinforced by the confrontation (which, of course, Anthony wins) between Anthony and the pagan philosophers.

But there are other aspects to the treatise that also shed light on the fourth century. Much of the conflict in which Anthony engages is physical. He wrestles with demons and fights off their (literal) physical attacks. This is significant on two fronts. First, it indicates a theology that externalizes the problems that Christians face: it is not so much sin, "the enemy within," as it is the external foe of the demonic that creates the dynamic in the Christian life. To a modern reader, this gives Anthony a somewhat two-dimensional feel: he is not so much a narrative hero with whom we can identify as he is a mythical figure who represents an ideal or a set of aspirations. Second, and more significant for the christological debates of the fourth century, it ties the portrayal of Anthony into the notion of *theosis* or "deification," which not only lies at the heart of Eastern Orthodox notions of salvation but which also drove the contemporary theological discussions of the time.

Put simply, deification emphasized the need for God to assume to himself human nature in order to bring that human nature into communion with God. In the incarnation, an ontological transformation of human nature was transacted which brought it to a level that had not previously been achieved, indeed, which had been frustrated by the fall into sin. This is the background to Athanasius's portrayal of Anthony: in ascribing godlike qualities to him, Athanasius is not, as might appear to modern Western readers, confusing Anthony with Christ; rather, he is portraying Anthony as the ideal man, a classic example of deification whereby his human nature has been raised to a level it would not have achieved if the incarnation had not taken place.

There are elements of this throughout the narrative: Anthony's body is described as remarkably fit and lean, right up to his death. Despite the lack of decent dentistry and the rough nature of his diet, his teeth do not fall out but are simply worn back to the gums. The beatings that the demons inflict upon him do only temporary and minimal damage to his body, which clearly possesses remarkable resilience and powers of restoration. Further, in more subtle allusions to the Bible, Anthony makes a garden in the wilderness, an implicit recapitulation of the garden of Eden, and indeed, in echoes of Elijah and John the Baptist, lives a life of asceticism in said wilderness. In other words, this is far more than the straightforward biography of a saint; it is itself a historical action that tells us much about the author and his world and theology.

The resonances with Elijah lead us to another aspect of the work: at his death, Anthony bequeaths his sheepskin to—guess who?—Athanasius. To extend the biblical reference, then, this is to make Athanasius himself the new Elisha, the one to whom Elijah left his cloak and double portion of his spirit. Anthony is therefore firmly co-opted for the Athanasian cause. This is no mere speculative piece of eisegesis: Anthony makes references in the *Life* to his opposition to the Arians, even using one of Athanasius's own favorite terms of abuse, *Ariomaniac*, to describe them. In addition, in his long speech, Anthony also warns against the Meletians, the followers of a schismatic group from the third century and, again, traditional enemies of Athanasius and his supporters.

All of this is to point to the fact that a text such as the *Life of Anthony* is so much more than a simple retelling of the life of a saint with a view to doing what the stated purpose in the prologue is: to encourage monks in their cause. In fact, it is also a conscious statement of theology and church politics in the fourth century, all of which are arguably within the recoverable intention of the author. Neither a simple acceptance of his stated intention, nor a flat reading of the text which demands that it be one thing rather than another is sufficient as a historical approach; and this is only possible when the reader is prepared to allow that the text may have a variety of purposes and is then familiar enough with the context to discern what those purposes might be.

There is one further element that can be added to this: those who know the fourth century are aware that the middle decades of this period witnessed the rise to prominence and power of bishops, and also the anchoring of much of their power in the growing monastic movement. Given this, the *Life of Anthony* can also be seen as illustrating the transition, with holy man Anthony effectively anointing Athanasius as his successor by the legacy of the sheepskin, and by this very notion reinforcing the link between monasticism and the episcopate. Again, reduction of the historical significance of the text to the stated intention of the author is to reduce the historical significance of the text to that of a mere didactic story.

In short, the historian needs to be wary of oversimplification and of defining the meaning of a historical action with reference to one single cause or intention. Historical actions are complex and require complex explanations; and this is why knowledge of context, as broad as we can make it, is critical. Further, the historian needs to understand that such complexity also means that, once again, any historical interpretation is provisional, not in the sense of, say, being necessarily susceptible to being shown to be false but in the sense of being a limited explanation. Who knows when a document might appear that sheds further light on Athanasius's *Life of Anthony*? It will not demonstrate that the treatise is not, in part, an anti-Arian tract because it clearly is; but it might well deepen and expand further our interpretation.

Post Hoc, Propter Hoc

Another common error to avoid is that of *post hoc, propter hoc*, or literally, "after this, because of this." In its most brutal and obvious form, this is the argument that because event B happened after event A, therefore there must be some causal connection between the two things. Sometimes there is no connection; other times the connection might be a whole lot more complicated than the historian has made it out to be.

Most of us are familiar with this kind of error from conversations in everyday life. "The economy collapsed after the Conservative/Labour/Republican/Democratic Party was elected last year" would be a common example. Economies are, of course, massive entities, and while changes can occur very suddenly in terms of a stock market crash or a run on the bank, the causes of such are usually complex (once again!) and medium- to long-term. For example, if you print too much money, you will generally stir up inflation, but not immediately; it takes time for the excess money to permeate the economic system and to drive up prices. Thus, while it is rather comforting to blame the politicians, and, indeed, often not inappropriate so to do, the fact that somebody was elected last week and then this week the retail price index goes up ten percentage points and the stock market collapses may not be directly linked.

Another example of this faulty argumentation might be Edward Gibbon's thesis that the decline and fall of the Roman Empire was directly linked to the rise of Christianity, which undermined the values on which Rome had been built. Certainly, there is an interesting coincidence of the two things; and the way in which theological disagreements came to embody deeper geopolitical problems within the later empire indicates that there is a relationship between Christianity and the collapse of the Roman imperial project. But is this relationship one of cause and effect?

One might argue that, on the contrary, Christianity actually helped prolong the Roman Empire beyond the point where it should have collapsed. By the beginning of the fourth century, the Empire was vast and its bureaucratic structure was becoming increasingly incompetent to manage the overall structure. The church, however, with its network of congregations and its powerbases in key population centers, offered both a bureaucratic framework and a potentially unifying identity or ideology. Thus, Constantine's conversion was a most opportune occurrence for Rome, as the boundary between Empire and church was to become increasingly blurred over the following century, symbolized perhaps most significantly by the election of Ambrose, governor of Liguria/Aemilia, as Bishop of Milan in 374—even before he had been baptized. The skills for church leadership and for political administration were now virtually one and the same.

Thus, while controversies did fragment the Empire and cause strains in coming years, the argument that Christianity destroyed the Empire is tendentious and, indeed, tenuous at best. The case needs to be documented; and it would seem at least at first glance that Gibbon's reading of the situation is neither the only, nor the most, plausible of the accounts that could be given. Just because the one event happened after the other does not imply a necessary connection between the two.

Another example of this kind of error is provided by the oft-touted claim that the Reformation led to capitalism, or at least dramatically fuelled its rise in the sixteenth and seventeenth centuries. Over the years, the argument has taken various forms, perhaps most famously in the thesis of Max Weber that capitalism, while not strictly caused by Protestantism (specifically Reformed, or Calvinistic, Protestantism) was yet dramatically facilitated by it because of alleged affinities between said Protestantism and the kind of values that were embodied in the most successful forms of capitalism.

Many questions can—and indeed have—been raised about the "Protestantism leads to or facilitates capitalism" theses. The most crude theses fail to take into account that capitalism developed prior to the Reformation: after all, it was the Junkers, German bankers, who were intimately involved in the funding arrangements that led to the indulgence crisis of 1517 which launched Luther on his path to fame. Then, in the Weberian form of the thesis, numerous problems are evident, not least the assumptions that are made about the relationship between ideas and social practices, assumptions that need to be argued rather than assumed. More seriously, however, Weber falls foul of the *post hoc propter hoc* problem because he focuses on one of the most obvious novel phenomena of the time, Protestantism, and connects it to the rapid growth of another phenomenon, capitalism. In fact, of course, the mere coincidence of the two things does not mean they are necessarily connected; rather, this needs to be demonstrated; and, indeed, the question needs to be asked whether it is the *Protestantism* of Protestantism (i.e., its specific ideological content) that makes it so conducive to capitalism or whether it is something else related to the phenomenon. For example, Protestantism and sectarianism frequently led to social marginality, from the sixteenth to the late nineteenth century. This could just as easily be responsible for the ethic that facilitates capitalism—strong group identity, loyalty, the need to work hard, the necessity to find means of survival outside of the bureaucratic elites and establishments, etc.—and is, of course, not restricted to Christians but also connects to Jews, who are scarcely irrelevant to the history of capitalism. The close chronological connection of the rise of Protestantism and the rise of capitalism is not in itself sufficient to posit a definite, direct link between the two things.

Of course, the *post hoc propter hoc* fallacy often contains some truth. Nobody would deny (as indicated above) that there is some connection between Protestantism and capitalism. The point is that the relationship between two phenomena is often more complicated than such simple connections allow. In others words, this can be yet another opportunity for oversimplification. Take, for example, the assassination of Archduke Franz Ferdinand by Serbian nationalists in Sarajevo in 1914. There was a time (probably long since gone) when every English schoolboy knew that this was the cause of the First World War. In a sense this claim was true: the assassination precipitated the diplomatic crisis which catapulted Europe into war. But in another sense it is wholly inadequate as an explanation: it only had the significance it did because of the elaborate set of alliances and treaties that then existed in Europe, because of the rise of German naval supremacy and because of the crisis in European imperialism, etc. It was the pretext for the conflict; but to describe it as the cause is to load it with freight that, frankly, it could not possibly bear all by itself.

In this context, it is perhaps worth bearing in mind a logical distinction between *necessary* causes and *sufficient* causes. A *necessary* cause is such that, if phenomenon B is present, then A must be present too; though the presence of A does not necessarily imply that B will occur. Thus, for Mrs. Thatcher to have been elected British Prime Minister in 1979, there must have been an election; but the fact that there was an election did not (at the time) necessarily mean that Mrs. T. would indeed become the prime minister. A *sufficient* cause is such that A necessarily implies the presence of B, but B could be caused by C; thus the presence of B does not mean that A is necessarily present. For example, Mrs. Thatcher could have been elected by a mass turnout of people who thought that blondes make the best politicians, but she could also have been elected because the majority of the British people in 1979 thought that the Conservative Party would run the country better than the Labour Party of James Callaghan; thus, Mrs. T.'s election did not necessarily imply a massive swing toward the political popularity of blondes in the British population.

This distinction is important in injecting a certain amount of modesty into our historical analyses and claims. To claim Protestantism as a cause of capitalism, or at least as a cause of its success and rapid development, is a claim which itself needs to be nuanced. To claim it as a necessary cause is to posit an essential connection between the two phenomena, such that flourishing capitalism can only really be caused and can only really prosper under the conditions created by Protestantism. To claim it as a sufficient cause, however, is considerably more modest, and is merely to point to the fact that elements of Protestantism are conducive to the development of elements of capitalism; but it does not create any hard and fast necessary connection between the two. I would suggest that the modesty of the sufficient cause is appropriate in such circumstances, and the distinction between the two types of cause needs to be constantly borne in mind lest one move unconsciously from claims about sufficiency to claims about necessity and commit a logical fallacy with potentially far-reaching effects.

The logical complexities of causation also usefully highlight for us the complexity of historical analysis. Take, for example, a car accident on the motorway. How many causes are there? Someone designed and built the road, presumably because other people wanted to travel efficiently between two or more places; someone designed and built the cars involved; individuals bought those cars; the same people decided to travel on that road at that time on that day; and one or more drivers were not concentrating at a particular point in time. All these causes are necessary, but not one of them, by itself, caused the crash. None of them is redundant in that all play their part, but taken in isolation, they do not allow us to make sense of the event of the crash. So it is with history: causality is a complicated thing, and the logical or chronological priority of one action over another does not mean we can reduce the relationship between the two things to simple cause and effect.

Thus, the historian must be wary of the temptation to simplify that this fallacy brings with it, and also of the temptation to read historical events and phenomena at a very superficial level, where two sequential historical phenomena are connected more in the mind of the historian than in actuality. Finally, historians must be wary of the tendency (as with Gibbon and with Weber) of reading their own presupposed conclusions into the evidence. This can only be done, as outlined earlier, by looking for counterevidence to any thesis, and also by asking questions concerning how a thesis can be verified.

Word-Concept

Another fallacy to which historians must not fall prey is confusing the word with the concept. We have already discussed one form of this in the chapter on anachronism, where I made the point that the use of a word, say, liberty or democracy, in a historical text does not mean that the author intended the same concept as someone using the same word today. What the historian has to do is understand how terms were normally used in accordance with the conventions of the period being studied.

There is another version of the fallacy, however, which denies that somebody can have a particular concept if they lack a particular word or phrase. A good example can be found in relation to the fourth century discussions of Trinitarian doctrine. Popular author Dan Brown, in his inexplicably popular bestseller, *The Da Vinci Code*, makes it sound as if the deity of Christ was an invention of the church in the fourth century and that the vote at Nicea was a close call. In fact, we know that the vote was overwhelmingly in favor of Christ's divinity (one might debate as to how representative the gathering was, or to what extent the emperor's menacing presence may have influenced the delegates, but one cannot debate the margin of victory). Thus, Brown is guilty of basic factual error; but he is also guilty of confusing the existence and acceptance of a specific creedal statement with the existence and acceptance of a concept. For instance, much work has been done by scholars such as Richard Bauckham on the evidence for the fact that the New Testament writers themselves believed that God was one, that Jesus was God, and that there was a distinction between Father and Son. That this concept was not formulated using the technical Greek vocabulary which was developed and refined during the fourth century in order to give it clear expression is undeniable; but that does not allow one to conclude that the basic concepts which the Nicene Creed was to articulate were not present prior to the coining of the creedal terminology.

The same point can also be made about a term that is often associated with the kind of theology developed by certain Protestant theologians in the seventeenth century, the covenant of redemption. This was language that appeared in the 1630s and 1640s among a number of Protestant Reformed theologians which expressed a fine point of doctrinal divinity by using the language of covenant to describe the eternal will of God in his plan of salvation, with particular reference to the Father appointing the Son as Mediator. It is a complex idea and comes to the fore rather suddenly at this particular point in time. The question then is: did the concept exist prior to the terminology? The obvious answer is, yes, of course. One can scarcely coin a term for a concept that does not exist. The historian's task is thus at this point one akin to that of an archaeologist: to find out how and why the term emerged at this point, and the answer, to put it in its simplest terms, is twofold: the language of covenant was increasingly prominent in Reformed theology, never more so than in the middle decades of the seventeenth century when it was used not simply in terms of theology but also of politics; and from the Reformation onward certain new emphases in discussions of the person and work of Jesus Christ had emerged in various theological systems that provoked both polemical discussion with Catholic theologians and, consequently, doctrinal and linguistic refinements within Protestantism. When these two trajectories are explored, it becomes clear that the concerns and indeed the basic doctrinal content of the covenant of redemption were there before the term itself was coined.

The Genetic Fallacy

Historians who commit the genetic fallacy are guilty of the error of allow-ing the origins of something to determine its current nature or mean-ing. I confess to having a particular soft spot for this fallacy because it is such a useful stick with which to beat the Americans, and no Englishman trapped in the former colonies should ever miss an opportunity to do that. Thus, I am always happy to remind American friends that, when things go wrong in the States, or politicians are shown to be venal and corrupt, this is exactly what one should expect from a nation which, in terms of its origins, is the result of an illegal colonial rebellion, orchestrated by a gang of rabble-rousers who had no respect for the established, legal, and God-given authorities set over them. A nation born in such circumstances is doomed to be a mess.

Of course, the argument is entirely fallacious. Whether America is a mess has nothing to do with the nature of its origins in the War of Indepen-dence. In any given chain of cause and effect (and by this point the reader should be aware that, in the writing of history, there is no such thing as a single, simple chain of cause and effect between two actions or events), it is not necessary that the originating cause be reflected in some later effect.

A causes B; B can cause C; C can cause D, or perhaps, replicate itself and cause another C. Imagine an election: candidate Smith rigs the election so that he wins by buying votes, but then he passes legislation that prevents anybody else from doing the same. Does that mean his legislation is corrupt and damaging in the effect it has, simply because he himself was a living contradiction of its principles? Or, to take an example from history, Alec Douglas-Home was appointed leader of the British Conservative Party in the 1960s, an era when leaders of said Party were not elected; rather, they "emerged" after high-level discussions of the Party's top brass. But he then went on to reform the Party's procedures in order to ensure that future leaders would be elected by the Tory members of Parliament. Clearly the virtues of the legislation (a more open, democratic process) were not undermined or rendered negligible by the fact that the mastermind behind the reform was himself the product and beneficiary of the old system that he was working to dismantle.

Many readers might well be thinking at this point that this fallacy is so obviously problematic that it cannot possibly have much force within the writing of history today. True, its flaws are obvious; but, in fact, it does enjoy considerable vogue in some quarters. Take, for example, the most radical wings of the Christian America movement where the argument is (*pace* my own favored use of the genetic fallacy) that America was founded by men motivated by and large by their commitment to the Christian faith and their desire to build a Christian nation. Thus, America was and is—or at least, ought to be—a Christian nation, and her founding documents embody Christian virtues. This leads to interpretations of the present that can engage simply in anachronistic value judgments on actions and events; or, perhaps in a more sinister way, connect America to events in biblical prophecy, God's providential plans for the world, etc.

Few would deny that America's founding documents embody civic virtues, though what makes those virtues distinctively Christian is surely rather debatable. Thus, the significance of the impact here is perhaps less on the actual writing of history than on the subsequent use of such history in contemporary politics; but it is useful to identify exactly what the underlying problem with such history is.

Generalization

Generalization is another area that can prove tricky for the historian. On one level, some generalization is necessary. For example, the statement, "The British were at war with the Germans between 1939 and 1945" is a general statement but is arguably not misleading or inaccurate. Anyone who knows the conventions of language will know that, despite what the sentence could appear to mean, given its use of the definite article—that every person of British nationality was at war during the stated time with every person of German nationality—this is not what is intended. Historians know that there were some of each nationality who were pacifists or perhaps even active supporters of the cause of the other nation, even to the point of being combatants. Other statements, such as "English people prefer tea to coffee," are also innocuous, given that only the most literal minded would see the statement as a claim about the warm beverage preference of every single son or daughter of England's green and pleasant land. Thus, when you reflect for any time upon the practice of historical writing, you will notice that generalizations abound and (if I can generalize here) frequently not only do no harm but are really quite necessary. The idea that one should have to list every individual British person alive between 1939 and 1945 and give a detailed analysis of his attitude to Germany between these dates in order to be able to make a meaningful statement about that period of time is self-evidently absurd.

The historian must, however, be careful with generalizations as they can, in some circumstances, prove very problematic. First, they can be used in a way that is connected to the problems of reification. Arguments built on national characteristics would seem to fall into this kind of category. Nineteenth-century histories, for example, will frequently speak of specific ethnic groups in terms of character or moral traits that are seen to be endemic to them. This is fallacious not simply because it frequently involves reification of race in a manner that is itself highly debatable (Is race to do with skin color? Eye shape? Hair? Language? Etc., etc.), but also because it connects this reified concept of race or, just as frequently and just as tendentiously, nationality, with moral behavior. Thus, we get the wily

Oriental who cannot be trusted, the fawning Uncle Tom, the sensuous and self-indulgent Turk, the humorless German who is mindlessly obedient to authority, the uptight and sneering Englishman, the honest but ignorant Scottish Highlander, and so on. Indeed, today it is American soap operas, more than historians, that tend to indulge such fantasies: is there a single character with an English accent who is not devious and implacably evil? And who has not become bored over the last few decades with hearing lectures from "celebrities" about how sound Eastern wisdom is and how awful Western thought has been. Such silliness really presupposes both a reification of something that does not really exist as such and the possibility of then generalizing from said reification.

A second problem with generalizing is that it can frequently lead the historian to make claims that are logically unsound, particularly in analogical arguments that move from one set of circumstances to another in order to draw inferences about the latter. Take, for example, the rise of totalitarianism in the first half of the twentieth century. Given the examples of Russia and of Germany, it would have appeared to many in the 1930s that liberal democracy was doomed: in Russia, a predominantly peasant-based economy simply collapsed into communism; in Germany, by contrast, a highly sophisticated economy also collapsed into a form of totalitarianism. For sure, there were profound differences between the two forms of totalitarian rule: Russia developed a state-owned economy, while private enterprise continued in Germany; the Nazis never developed the kind of surveillance state that at times virtually abolished private life in Stalin's Soviet Union. But in a sense, these differences reinforced the fact that while there could be dramatic local variations concerning economic context and political ideology, one thing seemed certain—democracy was in crisis and dying away, while totalitarianism represented the wave of the future. This is surely one of the reasons why so many intellectuals in the 30s tended toward fascism (as in the case of T. S. Eliot) or communism (as in the case of W. H. Auden): one had to choose the winning side, and the major argument about the future prospects for democracy was already decided.

Yet we now know that the triumph of totalitarianism was far from assured, and certainly not in the forms then on offer. Neither old-style Nazism/fascism or communism are regarded anymore as serious contenders for the title of "The Future's Most Promising Political System," and even new forms of totalitarianism, such as the religious regimes in places such as Iran, are constantly under pressure from democratic elements within their respective societies. This has a twofold implication. First, it has an immediate impact upon how we understand the future, in that we cannot and should not write history as if it is simply a case of identifying the inevitable phases of a society as it moves toward a predetermined goal. We looked at this in the chapter on explanatory schemes and saw that historians who write in such a way are usually riding for a serious fall.

Second, we need to be wary about producing general rules of historical development based upon the comparison of one group, society, or nation with another. What is interesting in history is the particular, the strange, the unexpected. Whether it is a novel use of a word or phrase in a particular text that breaks with established conventions, or whether it is the fact that while many societies seem to slide into totalitarianism, others find their democratic institutions to be strengthened by the same set of circumstances, it is the odd and the unusual that makes interesting historical analysis possible. In the mid-twentieth century, it was not the task of the historian to extrapolate from the experience of a couple of nations to produce or buttress some larger political philosophy of history; rather, it was the historian's task to ask why Nazism was such an effective force for terrible political change in Germany while British fascism was little more than a comic sideshow cast of a bunch of hooligans who liked walking around in black shirts, shouting at people. In other words, generalization can become problematic when it blinds us to the particulars of historical action.

Asking the Right Questions

One area where many historians fall down is in the framing of questions. A moment's thought indicates that we are all aware of how the framing of a question can shape the answer. For example, the old chestnut, "When did you stop beating your wife?" is a fine example of a question that effectively checkmates the interviewee, given that his answer must opt for one of two alternatives, both of which involve a confession of wife beating.

Historians are not immune to such problems. In the chapter on anachronism, we discussed the need to avoid imposing anachronistic categories of analysis on texts and periods of time. Often such anachronism emerges in the questions asked: Was Luther an anti-Semite (implying that the racial category of anti-Semitism was actually present as a concept in the sixteenth century)? Was Calvin a Calvinist (implying that the later collection of theological commitments known as "Calvinism," as forged in late sixteenth and early seventeenth-century polemics, can be brought into relation to Calvin's theology as a means of judging fidelity or otherwise to his thinking)? Both questions presuppose anachronisms in their very framing, which then present clear problems when trying to answer them.

The problem does not just involve anachronism, however; often, questions are clearly driven by particular ideological commitments that arguably lead to distorted answers. Take, for example, the old-fashioned English gentleman's habit of holding doors open for ladies. One could ask the following questions: Where did this practice originate? How do the men involved in this activity understand its significance? How do the women respond? All such questions are genuinely exploratory. But there are other questions that are perhaps not so straightforward, such as, what does this practice tell us about male chauvinism at the time? Or, how does this practice reflect oppression of women in England? Both of these questions come loaded with ideological freight that essentially assumes, or at least strongly points toward, a particular conclusion. Of course, one can answer "nothing" to the first and "it doesn't" to the second, but there is a certain gravitational pull away from such answers embedded in the questions themselves. The questioner seems rather to take it for granted that this practice *is* an example of male oppression of women and is therefore merely interested in *how* this is so. The question is thus political, not historical.

Those driven by particular philosophies as applied to history are particularly vulnerable to this kind of error. In addition to feminists, we might also think of Marxists, for whom evidence is ultimately analyzed through the grid of dialectical materialism. The question, how does this event reflect the class struggle? thus comes to supplant a less loaded question such as, does this event reflect the class struggle? which at least holds open the possibility that the framework of analysis might itself be subject to correction in light of the relevant findings.

This is not to say that all questions which are in some sense loaded are illegitimate. Take, for example, the following: How did German imperialism cause the First World War? One might respond by saying, well, that question seems to assume that German imperialism did cause the First World War. How is that different from the question about door opening and male oppression of women? I would argue it differs at a number of levels. First, the connection between German imperialism and the First World War is susceptible to the canons of historical verification. We can look at the evidence and establish whether there is a connection between these two very particular phenomena. Second, the question is not obviously linked to a particular political viewpoint. The categories in the question (imperialism, Germany, First World War) are not particularly political or philosophical. True, the question could be asked by a person with a specific ax to grind against the Germans or a vested interest in blaming the Kaiser for all the bloodshed; but in practice neither the question nor the range of answers likely to be given are necessarily wedded to an ideology in the way that questions about male oppression—a clearly philosophical or political category—are.

In sum, the historian needs to think not just about historical evidence but also about the kinds of questions that are posed in relation to the evidence. As always, there is the need to be self-critical, to see what ideological freight is contained within the questions themselves and how this may lead to certain conclusions.

Category Confusions

The error of confusing categories is common to many fields of discourse, not just history, and is summarized in the old saying about the impossibility of comparing apples and oranges. The error is simple: two things are compared or contrasted that are actually incomparable. Think, for example, of comparing the color red with a bucket of sand. There is no comparison because red is a color and a bucket of sand is a collection of tiny, stone-like granules. Or compare a mouse to an armchair. Again, there is no comparison in general terms because one is an animal, the other is a piece of furniture. One could compare aspects of the mouse to aspects of the chair—the color, for example, or the texture—but no blunt comparison of the two things is really feasible.

Given the rather obvious nature of the error as explained by these examples, it is perhaps surprising that it does occur within books by reputable historians. For example, I recently reviewed *Seeking a Better Country* by D. G. Hart and John R. Muether, which draws a contrast in an early chapter between seventeenth-century Puritanism and seventeenth-century Presbyterianism, a contrast which then shaped the analysis in the rest of the work.[3] The argument is that Puritanism represented a movement focused on religious experience while Presbyterianism was much more focused on traditional categories of church, doctrine, etc. The problem, of course, is that Presbyterianism is an identifiable, empirical category: there was an identifiable Presbyterian church in Scotland in the seventeenth century, and in England there were those who, though within the Anglican church, were committed to changing her polity to that of Presbyterianism. Puritanism, however, was not such an identifiable party; indeed, as noted above, it tends rather more in the direction of a scholarly construct, and not even scholars have reached a clear consensus on what exactly constituted a Puritan. Indeed, one thing scholars do agree on is that it was not a sign of ecclesiastical commitment in terms of the details of polity: there were Puritans who were moderate Episcopalians, Presbyterians, and Independents. In other words, to draw a contrast between the Puritan approach to something and that of the Presbyterians would be to commit a number of errors: first, one of reification in making Puritanism a single, definable entity; second, of generalization, in ascribing a single view to this reified phenomenon; and, last but not least, a category mistake in comparing apples and oranges. That is quite an impressive tally of fallacies for a single

[3] D. G. Hart and John R. Muether, *Seeking a Better Country* (Phillipsburg, NJ: P&R, 2007).

historical point. This kind of mistake, of course, is not confined to religious history: confusions between political philosophies (e.g., socialism) and the specific platforms of political parties (e.g., the Labour Party of Great Britain) can also be misleading and confusing. In short, when a historian makes comparisons or draws contrasts, she needs to make sure that the things in question are of like kind.

Is Providence an Explanation?

I end this chapter with a brief look at a favored explanation among religious folk for why things happen: it all comes down to providence. Of course, for a religious believer, committed to the notion of divine sovereignty (that God is in control of all things and that all things happen for a reason), the idea of providence would seem an attractive one for explaining historical actions and events. This has been a staple of religious literature over the years: early church martyrdom accounts are shot through with the idea that, whatever the suffering of the martyrs, God is in control and all is done for the greater good. In the sixteenth century, a Protestant martyrologist like John Foxe was able to read the history of the church through its sufferings, the so-called Trail of Blood, in order to demonstrate how God had preserved a true church during the Middle Ages. More recently, the claims by leading evangelicals such as Pat Robertson and Jerry Falwell that the 9/11 attacks were God's judgment on America for tolerating abortion and homosexuality are really rooted in the notion that the meaning of events is to be found by connecting them to God's providential oversight. This same view has recently been expressed in a more sophisticated way in a book on how to approach history from a Christian perspective, though here the reasons for God's perceived judgment are greed, free trade, and militarism.[4]

The problems with providential readings of history are manifold, but I will focus just on two. First, they attempt to explain particulars in terms of a universal, which is remarkably unhelpful in its limitations. Take the Twin Towers as an example: to say they fell down on 9/11 because of providence

---

[4]Steven J. Keillor, *God's Judgments: Interpreting History and the Christian Faith* (Downers Grove, IL: InterVarsity, 2007).

is really little improvement on saying that they fell down because of gravity. To claim the latter is to speak truth, but it is also to explain nothing about what really happened that day. Most believers in providence, when pushed, would agree that all things are providential; thus, if the Twin Towers had not been attacked that day, it would still have been providential. In other words, even if one regards divine providence as an ontological reality, it is really useless to the historian in trying to interpret historical events. The historian deals with particulars; providence is universal—and universal causes are of no great use in particular explanations.

The second problem with providential explanations is that they claim to read God's will off the surface of historical events in a glib and easy manner. In fact, what they really do is allow the historian to express his or her own particular philosophical or moral commitments in a way that is invulnerable to external criticism. Once the "God's providence" card is played, the argument is over. The Christian thinker who hates abortion is confronted by the outrage of 9/11 and uses the events as an opportunity for reinforcing his or her own moral understanding of the nation. The connection between the terror attacks and the nation's stand on abortion is not empirically verifiable; it exists solely in the mind of the interpreter. It is a gnostic connection to which others have no access. Indeed, another person sees it as a judgment on militarism and free trade. In each case, providence is wheeled in as a means of providing divine sanction for the interpreter's own political views. The interpretation itself cannot be verified because it offers an explanation that enjoys only a highly speculative connection to the empirical events.[5]

In short, providence may well be a sound theological doctrine, but it really has no place in the toolbox of the historian because it pushes the historian beyond the realms of what is and is not verifiable according the canons of evidence and interpretation.

---

[5] A Christian believer might object at this point that the Bible clearly offers providential interpretation of historical events; but the difference is surely that the Bible is regarded by Christians as both an authoritative account of events and an authoritative *interpretation* of those events, inspired by God. That is not the case, for example, with 9/11 and the various "Christian" interpretations offered in the aftermath.

Conclusion

I hope that this chapter has made the reader somewhat uncomfortable, for the study of common fallacies is often akin to looking into a mirror: as we look at the mistakes of others, sooner or later, we see our own reflections. As I look back on over two decades of serious historical study, I am acutely aware of the times when I have reified, indulged in anachronisms, engaged in the occasional category confusion, muddled up word and concept, and committed a host of other errors. Every historian makes mistakes; the important thing is to gain an understanding of why they are mistakes. Once that is done, they become much easier to avoid in the future.

Concluding Historical Postscript

In ending this small volume, I am conscious that I have barely scratched the surface of what it means to write history. We looked at Holocaust Denial as a way of seeing how and why evidence means something rather than nothing in particular. We looked at explanatory schemes and saw how, in the example of Marxism, there is often a fine line between an approach that facilitates explanation and one that prescribes meaning. We looked at anachronism in order to understand one of the perennial problems of engaging the past from the perspective of the present. And we looked at a smattering of other fallacies to which the unwitting historian can fall prey if not self-conscious about method. Here I want to reflect more generally upon the usefulness of history and the kind of things that one should be doing in order to be a better historian.

The Usefulness of History

The culture in which we live in the West exhibits powerful antihistorical tendencies, for a variety of different reasons. The dominance of science has led to an assumption that the present is superior to the past, and the future to the present. There is, of course, much truth to this: after all, who wants to go back to an era before analgesics, antibiotics, and flush toilets? And with medical care, is it not the case that every decade brings significant breakthroughs that mean that illnesses which once crippled or killed can now be cured in days by taking medication or undergoing routine surgery? The kind of a world that witnesses such developments inevitably tends to look to the future and away from the past for inspiration.

Closely related to this is the impact of technology within our world. In previous eras, technology, such as it was, often favored the aged and drew people's attention to the past. My mother lives in an old weaver's cottage in the Cotswolds, and the fireplace in the front room bears the marks where the weaver's loom would have been placed. In the mid-nineteenth century, it is likely that a child would have sat and watched his father weaving and learned how to use the technology, such as it was, by observing how the older generation used it. Today, when I visit my mother, more often than not I spend time trying to make today's technology, in the shape of a DVD player, work. But I find myself dependent upon the wisdom of a much younger niece to help me understand the various buttons and remote control units that need to be mastered in order to make the device do what I want. Technology now invests the young with wisdom and power and makes the old look inept and incompetent; and, once again, this serves to create a spirit of the age that is inimical to seeing the past as a particularly helpful source of wisdom.

It is not just science and technology that fuels the antihistorical culture and antihistory attitudes of the present day, however; capitalism and consumerism, built as they are upon innovation, constant re-creation of markets, and thus also the built-in obsolescence of commodities, also promote such values. Who wants yesterday's fashions? You might like to wear a John Travolta-style *Saturday Night Fever* white suit, but most of us prefer to dress in ways that connect with the present day rather than the disco fever of the mid-1970s. And while the mobile phone you owned in 1990 might well be just as effective at making calls as the one you bought this morning, the latter looks so much cooler, does so many more things (which you didn't even know you needed to do until the maker told you), and is so much lighter that there really is no comparison. You might, of course, buy a replica phone from the 1930s for your house, but that has less to do with your respect for history and more to do with a Humphrey Bogart nostalgia kick that you have been on since seeing him in *The Maltese Falcon* one Saturday night on Turner Classic Movies. And, of course, the technology inside said phone will include state-of-the-art microchips; you will not have to hand-wind it as Bogey did.

Finally, as has been alluded to at a number of points in this book, there is the other aspect of antihistorical thinking, and that is the more sophisticated critical attitude that sees all writing of history as essentially propaganda designed to justify certain political stands in the present, primarily political stands favored by white, heterosexual, Western males. Add to this a suspicion about the ability of language to convey meaning and a suspicion that authors—all authors—are out to manipulate their readers, and the writing of history looks like a murky and disreputable trade indeed.

In fact, as I hope has been clear in the preceding chapters, I regard the claim that history is nothing but political propaganda as highly contentious and as claiming more than it can prove. As I argued in chapter 1, even the fact that something is written with bias and with an agenda does not mean that it cannot be subjected to agreed procedures of historical verification and logical falsification. It is one thing to claim that my statement that "Benedict Arnold was a damnable traitor to the American cause" indicates bias on my behalf, but quite another to claim that it therefore has no more merit as a statement of history than "Benedict Arnold was a six-foot pink bunny from Wonderland."

As to the cultural insignificance of history, I would argue that the forces outlined above are powerful, but that does not mean they are correct. It is certainly sobering to be on a long flight, as I was recently, and to tune in to the "classic movies" channel on the in-flight entertainment and find nothing there older than the first of the X-Men pictures. Classic for me means at least pre-1960, and probably really pre-1955 (and black-and-white to boot!); it seems that few today have cultural memory banks (and thus

171

historical sensibilities) that go back beyond the last decade. What hope can there be, therefore, for the writing and teaching of history?

Being something of a contrarian, the very contempt with which history is held in today's society is sufficient motivation for me to be interested in it, but in fact there are more and better reasons than a simple desire to swim against the tide. An understanding of history is crucially important to a rounded understanding of the present. One of the things that (I hope) the earlier chapters in this book have helped bring out is the truism that the present is profoundly shaped by the past at every level. That may seem obvious, but it is amazing how often we can forget this simple fact and assume that what we have today is nature, not culture, and that the way we think and do things is simply the correct way that has emerged at last. We tend, if you like, always to think of ourselves as the Last Men, and our times as the End of Time. Sure, there may be improvements in medicine and technology to come, but we have essentially arrived.

In this context, the study of history can have many healthy and sobering effects that, far from merely offering justifications of the status quo, as many postmodern thinkers seem to fear, actually enable us to have a critical handle on the way things are. Sometimes there are obvious lessons to be learned: the Holocaust, for example, reveals that, yes, human beings, and very ordinary human beings at that, are capable of performing the most horrific and violent acts against others, sometimes even former friends and neighbors. Indeed, the various studies of "the banality of evil," to use Arendt's appropriate though now somewhat hackneyed phrase, serve to remind us that if one of the most technologically and culturally sophisticated nations in Europe can descend rapidly into such bestiality, then there is no room for any of us to be complacent.

Yet there are more subtle lessons too. One notable thing about immigrating to a foreign country is that the very difference of the culture to which one moves allows one to see both the idiosyncrasies of one's new culture and of that from which one has departed. When one only ever lives in one culture, the assumption is that everything one sees and experiences is nature, the norm, and that everybody else, to the extent that they do not conform, is deviant, subnormal, etc. Cross-cultural experience is excellent for disabusing one of such instincts.

History can be like that: not everyone has the opportunity to live for extended periods as a guest in another's culture, but history confronts the student with a different time and a different place, where people think, act, and behave in different ways. In this manner, rather like immigration, we come to understand the forces and influences that shaped the way the world was in the past, and hopefully we become more aware of the way in which forces previously unnoticed and invisible shape and guide the present.

To take a trivial example: I grew up near the Welsh border in England. I knew that the Welsh, as a people group, not necessarily as individuals, did not like the English and vice versa; I assumed this was natural. And I, naturally, disliked the Welsh, particularly their rugby team. Only later, as I came to understand the histories of the two countries, socially, politically, and economically, and as I also began to grasp the significance of other factors—the importance of geographical proximity in heightening ethnic rivalries, for example—did I come to understand that the comedy of, say, Welshman Max Boyce was not simply a reflection of the ontology of the West of Britain but was actually a cultural artifact that had a history lying behind it; and that the Anglo-Welsh rugby rivalry was the product of historical processes, not a genetic quirk.

The same is true for understanding almost any aspect of the modern world. One cannot begin to understand the conflict in the Middle East without understanding such things as the role of the British Empire, the impact of the Holocaust, the importance of oil, etc. One cannot understand the rise of militant Islam (surely the greatest surprise of all to those, like myself, weaned on the general theories of secularization that abounded in the twentieth century) without understanding the Western imperialism of the nineteenth and twentieth centuries, and the way in which religion has often functioned in history as an idiom for forging political and ethnic identities or of resisting dominant, secular powers.

Of course, what applies at these macro levels also applies at a local level: aspects of my own thought and behavior become more comprehensible in light of historical study. I have already mentioned my childhood antipathy to the Welsh rugby team, but many other things in my life, from taste in music to personal political convictions, are all more comprehensible in the light of wider historical factors. How many of us feel the need to keep on buying things, or to replace things that work perfectly OK with the latest models and design? Why do we do this? Well, an understanding of the way capitalism has developed and behaved, along with its ancillaries such as the advertising industry, the rise of disposable income, the invention of leisure time, etc., all have their part to play; and a good grasp of history thus helps me to understand my own behavior.

In short, I believe we have a choice. We can ignore history, and thus doom ourselves to understanding our own small world as reflecting nature, just the way things are, and by so doing doom ourselves to be enslaved to the forces around us that remain unseen but which nonetheless exert a powerful pressure on us. Or we can study history, and in so doing, simultaneously relativize ourselves and our times and, ironically, somewhat liberate ourselves in such a way that we understand more of our world and how we fit into it. Only the man who knows the forces that shape the way he thinks is capable of resisting those forces; and history is a great help in identifying and exposing such hidden things.

Training to Be a Historian

Every year, students come to my office and ask what they need to do to be better historians. This is in some ways a tough question. One of the great delights of history is surely its interdisciplinary nature. Even in the brief pages of this book, we have encountered a number of different types of history: economic, political, social, and intellectual. All are legitimate, and all have their own particular methods and approaches to the subject of the past. To be a good historian requires knowing a number of different fields. Thus, for those who have read this book and are inspired to continue with their historical studies, I would suggest that the first thing to do is to read as widely as possible, both in the field of history and in other areas.

It is my firm conviction that a good historian is a good historian, no matter what the period under discussion. The same procedures of evidence identification, verification, interpretation, and narrative construction apply whether one is studying the Roman Republic, the Crusades, the Reformation, the Industrial Revolution, the rise of popular culture, or the changing nature of the family in the twentieth century. The student of history at college level or beyond will no doubt have particular areas of interest and expertise, but the more widely he or she reads in history, the better the basic grounding in method and approach will be.

In doing this, it is key to read history books in a twofold way. First, and obviously, read them for what the historian *says*. I have just finished an excellent book, *Troublesome Young Men* by Lynne Olson, on the group of young MPs who helped to bring Winston Churchill to power in 1940.[1] In doing so, I learned a tremendous amount about the period, about the way the British Parliamentary system works, and other incidental matters, such as the disdain typically felt by war combatants for those who have never been in the front line of a military conflict. Indeed, I was struck by how the appeasers of the 1930s were generally not veterans of the First World War, while the anti-appeasement men were all graduates of the trenches. This was, for me at least, eye-opening and counterintuitive, as I had imagined those who had experienced such bloody combat would be the very men who would be gun-shy when it came to further conflict. Thus, the book taught me a lot about a period that I have never studied in any depth.

Having said this, there was another dimension to the way I read the book: I read it also to see what the historian *does*. The book contains a lot of references to letters, to parliamentary records, to radio broadcasts, and to memoirs written by the various protagonists. As I read the book, I was constantly reflecting on the kind of evidence Olson was marshalling, how she was interpreting it, how she connected the different kinds and quality of material, when and how she introduced broader background information, and how she synthesized all of this into a grand narrative that made sense of the events. To the extent I was able, from reading elsewhere, I also noted what she omitted, how firm her conclusions were,

[1] Lynne Olson, *Troublesome Young Men* (New York: Farrar, Straus, and Giroux, 2007).

the extent to which she was aware of how much was speculation and how much was directly connected to evidence, etc. In this way, I learned not simply about the period in question, but I also learned something about how a particular historian goes about her business. I also noted one or two strange explanations for things that should have been obvious to any British person—for example, an outline sketch of how the parliamentary whip system functions and a statement to the effect that British "public schools" were very expensive and private affairs—which indicated to me that the author was probably not British (she is actually American). All the time, I was reading the work critically, trying not simply to increase my knowledge of the early days of the Second World War, but also to learn better how to do history.

Thus, the first thing that any budding historian should do—indeed, that any professional historian should do—is read as much history as possible, not only to increase one's general supply of historical knowledge, but to see how other historians go about handling evidence and constructing narratives. We live at a wonderful time for doing this, when even Main Street booksellers carry a range of well-written, popular but thoughtful historical books that are delightful to read and inexpensive. The names of Niall Ferguson, Simon Schama, Orlando Figes, Robert Conquest, Amity Shlaes, and Barbara Tuchman should be staples on everyone's reading list.

The second thing historians should do is familiarize themselves with the culture of the place and period in which they are interested. I found this out in my studies of seventeenth-century Reformed theology by looking at the library catalogs of the men whom I was studying. They did not just read theology; they read widely in the history and literature of their own day. It makes sense, of course: no writer is simply a brain on a stick or a mere collection of synapses and electromagnetic impulses. Each is a real human being, living in a real time and a real place, as impacted by the wider context as much as anyone else; and the historian needs to understand that wider world.

Thus, when I teach a course on medieval theology, I encourage my students to read cultural histories of the medieval period as well as some of the literature of the time. In other words, in my class you would not only be expected to read Thomas Aquinas; I would hope that you would also read Geoffrey Chaucer and Dante. If ever I were to teach on religious thought in the modern period, I would not want students to study just Karl Barth; I would want them to read Sartre and Camus, see some movies by Ingmar Bergman, and, of course, look at the wider elements of popular culture, from novels to TV programs, to understand the wider cultural trends and currents in which the chosen authors were operating. This would enable students to have a better grasp of the broader contours of life and thought than would be supplied simply by studying a few isolated texts. As we noted earlier, only by so doing can we, for example, come to understand what is conventional in a particular text and what is exceptional and extraordinary. This is why we know that Luther's later writings against the Jews were fairly typical of his day and not the unique contribution to German culture that writers like William Shirer implied them to be.

Third, I encourage students to read widely in other genres of history and other disciplines beyond those of their immediate interest. History is eclectic, and as noted repeatedly in this study, it embraces a variety of different subgenres; and the historian's training and approach should reflect that eclecticism. It is important that the historian of ideas understands something of economics; that the economic historian understands something of the nature of literary texts; that the social historian understands something of the way in which ideas can function in a social setting, etc. Thus, it is vital for the historian to obtain a broad grounding in all different types of disciplines. The rule of thumb is: if it helps to explain human behavior, it is important for the historian to know something about it. I have warned of the danger of reducing historical explanation to a single cause ("It's all down to class struggle!" "It's all down to the perverted ideology of Hitler!" "It's all down to the impact of immigration!"), and so we must be aware that the complexity of human action requires an equally complex explanation that draws on various relevant disciplines.

Of course, each of these areas—economics, literary theory, sociology—is its own specialized discipline, and there is only so much that the hard-pressed historian can do in these fields. Yet a little energy expended in broadening horizons in such disciplines can pay dividends when it comes

177

to interpretation. For example, one does not have to read very far in literary theory before one becomes acutely aware that the issue of genre is crucial to the interpretation of a text, and that it is really rather basic to any historical analysis. Further, it may be hard to accept in a day of easy credit and instant gratification, but history is a discipline at which one expects to become better over the years precisely because one is always learning and improving and developing new and better perspectives. I remember being told at college that mathematicians had usually done their best work by the time they were thirty; the brain simply becomes less adept at creative mathematical thinking as the years go by. With history, this is not the case: the knowledge base and the techniques for doing history are not time-sensitive in the same way, and the more you know and the more widely you read, the better you potentially become as a historian. Not all things can be learned overnight, and the writing of good history is one of them. Few, if any, historians of note do better work in their twenties than they do in their forties and fifties. Like fine wines and Scotch whisky in the barrel, historical knowledge, technique, and literary style should all improve with age.

Next, historians need to have a good grasp of the history of their own discipline. This should go without saying. Committed as we are as a breed to understanding all actions as taking place in historical context, and as standing against the background of a prehistory, we must not exempt our own work from such. There are two ways to do this, both of which I would argue are necessary. First, we should read the great works of classic history: Herodotus's *Histories*; Thucydides's *History of the Peloponnesian War*; Tacitus's *Annals*; Eusebius's *Ecclesiastical History*; Polydore Vergil's *Anglica Historia*; John Foxe's *Acts and Monuments*; Giambattista Vico's *New Science*; Edward Gibbon's *The History of the Decline and Fall of the Roman Empire*; and so on. The student of history should be familiar with these and more in order to see how the task of the historian has been understood and executed throughout history. Much of modern history takes its cue from the methods defined by Leopold von Ranke in the nineteenth century, who emphasized empirical evidence and verification, but reading earlier writers is instructive for seeing how the discipline has changed and been refined over the years.

Second, historians should read histories of history in order to give themselves a context. There are numerous books on this subject available, quite often focusing on the current malaise in the discipline thanks to the inroads of excessively skeptical postmodern literary theory, but there are also some good solid introductions to the subject that avoid lunacy and offer helpful narrative accounts of the rise and development of the discipline. An older classic is R. G. Collingwood's *The Idea of History*; a more up-to-date work is Ernst Breisach's *Historiography: Ancient, Medieval, and Modern*.[2] Reading a work such a Breisach is helpful in understanding how and why historians today think and operate as they do.

Finally, I recommend that students read books on how to do history. Caution needs to be used here, as so much of the writing on how to do history is written not by historians but by philosophers. Indeed, there are those who have made careers out of writing books on how to do history but have never written any themselves (names are withheld to protect the guilty). Yet there are good books that outline the basic methods and procedures of the discipline, and it is always useful for the historian to have engaged in some critical self-reflection and have some grasp of relevant philosophy in order to pursue the task in a more self-aware manner. The three books that I would recommend in this context are as follows:

+ Quentin Skinner, *Visions of Politics I: Regarding Method*.[3] Skinner is a historian of ideas who has dedicated his life to reclaiming intellectual history from being a surreptitious way of contemporary dogmatizing and to advocating an approach that, rather like Reformation historian Heiko Oberman, studies ideas in context and produces a "social history of ideas." As we saw above, his

---

[2] R. G. Collingwood, *The Idea of History* (New York: Oxford University Press, 1956); Ernst Breisach, *Historiography: Ancient, Medieval, and Modern* (3rd ed., Chicago: University of Chicago Press, 2007).
[3] Quentin Skinner, *Visions of Politics: Regarding Method*, vol. 1 (Cambridge: Cambridge University Press, 2002).

methodological writings are particularly helpful in enabling the historian to be aware of, and to avoid, anachronisms.

+ Joyce Appleby, Lynn Hunt, and Margaret Jacob, *Telling the Truth about History*.[4] These three historians trace the recent history of the discipline and offer critiques of both the radical relativist left and the hard empiricist right. This is not so much a technical book on historical method as a polemical history of method.

+ Richard J. Evans, *In Defence of History*.[5] Evans, whom we met as the expert witness in the Lipstadt-Irving trial, defends his strongly empiricist approach to history. A tome in the tradition of the method of Ranke, it is perhaps the single most helpful volume on how to *do* history currently available.

The student of history who wishes to pursue the discipline at any decent level should purchase and read all three of these books.

Thus, the secret to becoming a better historian is really no secret at all: be aware of the various errors and fallacies noted in this book; read widely in the discipline; as you do so, ask not simply what is being said, but how the historian is going about the work of saying it; read widely in the culture of your chosen period; read eclectically across the disciplines, pillaging anything from other fields of intellectual endeavor that might help you understand the complexity of human action; read the classics of history; know the history of your discipline; and read sane accounts, by proven historians, of how they themselves pursue their craft. When you have done all this, you will find that you are a better historian than when you started.

Intellectuals and academicians tell us repeatedly that history has fallen on hard times. Certainly there are powerful cultural forces at work that would militate against the discipline. Yet the appetite for history books seems as strong as ever, if the shelves in local bookshops are anything to go by. History, when done well, is one of the most exciting, entertaining,

---

[4]Joyce Appleby, Lynn Hunt and Margaret Jacob, *Telling the Truth about History* (New York: Norton, 1994).

[5]Richard J. Evans, *In Defence of History* (London: Granta, 1997).

and stimulating activities in which we can engage. Understanding the past helps me to understand myself; understanding the world of yesterday serves to clarify my understanding of the world of today. It is my hope that this little book will serve to ignite that interest in others, to guide them away from dead ends and methodological mistakes to fruitful and creative avenues of approach, and to help in some small way the next generation of those who wish to make the past come alive for future generations. The past is indeed a foreign country; and it is well worth a visit precisely because of that fact.

APPENDIX

The Reception of Calvin: Historical Considerations

In addressing the reception of the thought of John Calvin from a historian's perspective, it is necessary first to reflect on exactly to what "reception" refers. Such conceptual clarity is an important prolegomenon to the work of history proper, lest historical analysis be skewed by inappropriate questions or frameworks.

First, *reception* is not the same thing as translation or mere replication of ideas. Given the status of Latin as the *lingua franca* of the educated classes, vernacular translations give some indication of the penetration of theology to a more popular audience, but they are no safe guide to *reception* of texts and ideas, a concept I take to have a twofold reference: first, to the way in which Calvin's texts were received, used, and transmitted by contemporaries and in subsequent generations; and, second, to the way in which his ideas were adopted, adapted, and developed by other thinkers.

In light of this, a further preliminary comment needs to be made, not so much about the reception of Calvin, perhaps, as about the reception of the kind of historical revisions proposed by, among others, Richard Muller and

Willem Van Asselt. There has been a tendency to understand the transformation of historical perspectives on Calvin and Reformed Orthodoxy
over the last three decades in terms of a "continuity thesis." This is built
on an understanding of the rejection of the historiography of the older
scholarship, which posited a series of fundamental breaks or discontinuities between the thought of Calvin, or the pre-Tridentine Reformers, and
the later, more confessionally-articulated theology of the Reformed in the
latter part of the sixteenth and the seventeenth centuries. Instead, so the
argument goes, Muller and company have offered a "continuity thesis," which
stresses the continuities between the earlier and later Reformed.

The problem with this understanding of the more recent scholarship is
that it fails to address exactly which changes would constitute "continuities"
and which "discontinuities" over a given period of time. For example, one
historian might well regard the differing formulations of the particularity
of the atonement in Calvin and, say, John Owen as still standing in continuity with one another; another theologian might see them as opposed, yet
both scholars might still agree on the ways in which the latter formulation
was a development of the other, their opinions of the *legitimacy* of such a
development being a function of their own theological commitments, or
even aesthetic tastes. In other words, the "continuity thesis" interpretation
or application of the newer scholarship, just like the old "discontinuity
thesis," might still be at root an anachronistic imposition of later doctrinal
judgments on historical texts. History serves dogma, as before.

Instead, I would suggest that the newer scholarship represents an
attempt to approach the texts as historical actions, and that questions of
continuity or discontinuity need to be set aside, or at least adopted in a
highly qualified form, in the assessment of the reception of theologians such
as Calvin by the later tradition. Texts are actions; and thus the questions
brought to bear on actions have to do, first and foremost, with context, as it
is context that provides the conventional framework within which actions
can be understood. And such context has two aspects: the synchronic and
the diachronic, the latter of which is the one to which the "continuity thesis"
largely pertains. Cast in this light, the question of reception of Calvin by
later generations is not, "Does this or that idea, expression, argument, or

text stand in continuity with Calvin's thought?" but rather, for example, "Does the reading of Calvin impact the way this writer reads this biblical text?" and "How is this writer using this idea or text of Calvin in his own situation?" To ask these questions is to avoid the questions that drove the older scholarship to its anachronistic conclusions.

Given all this, questions of continuity are perhaps best conceived of in three ways. First, there is the straightforward continuity of doctrine upon which all would probably agree. Thus, there is continuity between Calvin and later Orthodoxy on the issue of the hypostatic union of the divine and human in Christ. Here, the language used by Calvin, his predecessors, and his successors enjoys a basic stability, and there is little or no question concerning the continuity. In this context, however, it is perhaps better to think of continuity more in terms of confessional and catechetical documents than the writings of individual authors which enjoy no official ecclesiastical status. In other words, the continuity is confessional.

Second, there is a continuity of philosophical framework. Here, recent scholarship has done a great service by pushing back behind the rhetoric of Calvin and company about scholasticism and Aristotelianism to the way in which Calvin actually related to the wider medieval background, both in terms of method and basic philosophical schools. The result has been a picture of Reformation theology in general, and of Calvin in particular, that reveals the underlying debt to ongoing patterns of philosophical and academic discourse that were not as radically transformed by the Reformation as the ecclesiastical crisis would at first seem to imply. This needs to be kept always in mind when assessing the reception of Calvin.

Third, there is continuity in terms of problems or questions. In this sense, for example, one can argue that the later development of the covenant of redemption is continuous with Calvin, not on the grounds that Calvin held the idea in some embryonic or conceptual form that later generations merely made explicit or for which they developed a specific term; rather, it is continuous on the grounds that it addresses, in part, the problems raised by Calvin's stress upon Christ as Mediator according to both natures. The same approach can also be used in terms of the rise of the covenant of works, given the dependence of this structure on notions of Adam's representative headship of the human race, the impossibility of the finite creature making the infinite Creator a debtor, the rise of linguistic studies relative to the concept of covenant in Scripture, etc. Thus, while Calvin does not articulate a covenant of works concept, it can clearly be seen that those who do so stand in continuity with him in terms of the various problems that he faced and various positions he held. He did not create the covenant of works idea, but he helped feed into the tradition that ultimately produced the concept and the term.

Thus, if continuity is conceived of in these ways, we can avoid the kind of anachronism, or subordination of history to contemporary theological polemic, that is all too tempting for those involved in the task of historical theology.

In this context, a number of other comments need to be made. We have already noted a distinction within the idea of reception. First, there is reception of specific texts: translations, quotations, and marginal references would qualify as the raw data of such reception. For the historian, such reception is relatively easy to map, given the empirical nature of such. Quotations, marginalia, and attributed allusions all allow the historian to see a point of reception and then to address the matter of how Calvin's thought or writing is being received at precisely that point. For example, we now know from the recently edited minutes of the Westminster Assembly that Calvin was frequently quoted in the various debates. Influence is thus obvious and direct; and the nature of the reception of his thought and his writings on various points should be a relatively straightforward matter to discern.

The other type of reception, of ideas and concepts, is far more difficult to analyze; and this is particularly problematic when it comes to Calvin. The main reason for this, of course, is that Calvin's theology is not original with him but represents rather the expression of a number of traditions that neither originated with him nor were made confessionally normative by him or his writings.

It is worth noting that such reception can only be assessed with any accuracy when the ideas are so unique as to be traceable to a single unique source or where peculiar linguistic forms might be used that seem to originate with Calvin. Such is simply not the case with the vast majority of Calvin's theology. In this context, we have been ill-served by the term "Calvinism" and its cognates, with its implication that Calvin had a unique doctrinal status and made unique doctrinal contributions; even more so has the identification of the four heads of Dordt as the five points of Calvinism proved a hindrance to understanding Calvin's place in the intellectual development of Western theology. Indeed, the whole reification of "Calvinism" as a body of doctrine positively and uniquely connected to a single individual is counterproductive to careful historical analysis.

For a start, it is always worth remembering that theology, as a pedagogical discipline, is somewhat communal in nature. Luther is a great example of this: his early interactions with Karlstadt in the revival of Augustine's thought at the University of Wittenberg, and then his later collaborations with others, especially Melanchthon, all point to the fact that Reformation theology emerged from the communal settings of universities, academies, and churches. The difficulty of isolating the intellectual (as opposed to textual) contribution of one person from another is fraught with difficulties, as demonstrated by the disastrous attempts of the Finnish school of Lutheran studies to set Luther and Melanchthon at odds with each other on the issue of justification. It is surely the same with Calvin: his colleagues in Geneva, his many correspondents, and the many authors he read all inevitably fed into and shaped his thinking and made his theology something less than a unique contribution. Pardon the pun, but his thinking lacked a certain aseity on all of its major points.

Take, for example, predestination, perhaps the most notorious of Calvin's teaching in the popular mind. Of course, we all know that Calvin's teaching was not unique, but that he stood within an ongoing Western anti-Pelagian tradition that stretched back to Augustine himself. The last half century of scholarship has seen this basic point—that anti-Pelagianism was alive and well throughout the Middle Ages—time and time again. Now, anti-Pelagianism was not monolithic and did contain a certain variety of emphases and even diversity of specific positions, but not even Calvin's promotion of double predestination was a novel development in his own writings. There are occasional hints of the same in Augustine, and it is certainly to be found in medieval predecessors such as Thomas Bradwardine and John Wyclif, and in his contemporaries, Martin Luther being only the most obvious. In the wake of the Bolsec affair, Calvin's position was institutionalized and made normative in Geneva and its environs, and thus there is a clear legislative aspect of the reception of Calvin on this point; but on the broader theological plain, unless a writer specifically cites Calvin as a source, it is impossible to discern influence with any great certainty.

Having said this, it is of course interesting that Calvin, like Luther, uses predestination as a means of securing the believer's assurance of salvation, not an idea that enjoys significant precedent in the medieval anti-Pelagian tradition. Thus, this raises what one might call a double-reception question: how does Calvin use the medieval heritage for a new pastoral purpose, and then how is the Reformers' (plural) new use of this received and developed in the subsequent tradition? What problems does the Reformation use raise? What possibilities does it offer in other areas of doctrinal and pastoral concern?

One might also point to the *extra Calvinisticum* as a possible means whereby reception could be traced. Certainly, the name implies a certain origin in the thought of Calvin; but, of course, the terminology was originally coined by Lutheran polemicists with a vested interest in highlighting the novelty of Calvin's christology with reference to his understanding of the Lord's Supper. The fact that one can find similar christological constructs throughout church history, with thinkers such as Athanasius and Aquinas being only the most obvious, points to an immediate question of how much "extra" was actually involved in the "calvinisticum." Of course, Calvin's use of the idea relative to the Lord's Supper, and his somewhat mystical language regarding union within the context of the sacrament, are perhaps more indicative of a unique contribution; and thus there may be opportunity in the strict area of the use of language and metaphor to see whether, how, and where his forms of expression on this point were received by contemporaries and later generations. But that requires careful parsing both of Calvin's thought and of the tradition to which he is seen to have contributed.

Conclusion

The relation of Calvin to later Reformed theology is complex, not least because of the models of approach to the questions that have been offered in the past. Notions of discontinuity and continuity need to be carefully parsed if they are to be useful in addressing the various questions surrounding this topic and, even then, are only of comparatively limited usefulness.

Further, the myth of Calvin's originality is also a matter that needs to be overcome. Because Calvin made so little in the way of original theological contribution in terms of raw content, it is difficult to trace the reception of his thought in any detail among subsequent writers. Where explicit reference is made to texts, where quotations are offered, or where specific arguments are cited, then we have clear evidence with which to work. Beyond that, however, we need to tread carefully in this matter and not claim reception or influence in any stronger fashion than the very generic nature of much Reformed theological writing in the sixteenth and seventeenth centuries will allow us to do.

Still, as a final comment, we should not allow this to disturb us. That Calvin was buried in an unmarked grave tells us much about how he viewed his own significance in the grand scheme of things; and that he was chief prosecutor of Michael Servetus tells us all we need to know about how much Calvin himself valued original and unique contributions to theology in his day.

Index

Adamson, John, 103
Albert the Great, 144
Ambrose, 132, 153
Appleby, Joyce, 180
Aquinas, Thomas, 128, 144, 188
Arendt, Hannah, 58
Aristotle, 125–26, 144–46
Athanasius, 53–54, 148–51, 188
Auden, W. H., 82, 161
Augustine, 116, 187

Barth, Karl, 116, 177
Bauckham, Richard, 157
Bizer, Ernst, 145
Bloch, Marc, 122
Boethius, 144
Bownd, Nicholas, 92
Boyce, Max, 173
Bradwardine, Thomas, 188
Breisach, Ernst, 179
Brown, Dan, 157
Bucer, Martin, 123–24

Bullinger, Heinrich, 65
Bunyan, John, 90–91, 101, 103
Bush, Jeb, 16

Calvin, John, 23, 116, 120–29, 139, 163, 183–89
Cartledge, Paul, 14–15
Carto, Willis, 47–48
Chamberlain, Neville, 113
Charles I, 87, 95
Churchill, Winston, 37, 175
Clifford, Alan C., 145
Collingwood, R. G., 179
Constantine, 153
Cromwell, Oliver, 88–89

Davis, Robin, 48–50
Domitian, 78
Douglas-Home, Alec, 159

Edward I, 132
Eichmann, Adolf, 31–32, 58–59

Eliot, T. S., 161
Engels, Friedrich, 82
Enns, Peter, 27
Erasmus, 66
Eusebius, 178
Evans, Richard, 27, 32, 55, 61, 67, 73, 180

Falwell, Jerry, 166
Ferdinand, Franz, 154
Ferguson, Niall, 104
Fischer, David Hackett, 141
Foxe, John, 166, 178
Frege, Gottlob, 125, 144
Freud, Sigmund, 26
Froschauer, Christoph, 94
Fukuyama, Francis, 70, 105n

Gibbon, Edward, 152–53, 178
Grobman, Alex, 33, 35, 44

Hart, D. G., 165
Hartley, L. P., 109

Index

Hegel, G. W. F., 83–85
Herodotus, 178
Heydrich, Reinhard, 59–61
Hill, Christopher, 21, 30, 87–107
Himmler, Heinrich, 58, 60–61
Hitler, Adolf, 60–61, 71, 113–14, 137
Hobsbawm, Eric, 30, 87
Homer, 70
Hooper, John, 65–66
Hopkins, Keith, 14
Horthy, Miklós, 60
Höss, Rudolf, 58
Hume, David, 144
Hunt, Lynn, 180

Irving, David, 18–19, 27, 30, 32–33, 61–62

Jacob, Margaret, 180
James I, 92, 95
Jeckeln, Friedrich, 61
Jefferson, Thomas, 110, 147
Jenkins, Keith, 55

Kant, Immanuel, 143–44
Kennedy, John F., 99

Lenin, Vladimir, 86
Leuchter, Fred, 40–44, 47, 51
Lipstadt, Deborah, 18–19, 32–33, 61
Locke, John, 110
Lukacs, John, 26, 69
Luke, 80–81
Luther, Martin, 65, 92, 111, 125–26, 129–40, 154, 163, 187–88

Marx, Karl, 26, 82–87
McCalden, David, 47–48
Melanchthon, Philip, 65, 145, 187
Millet, Paul, 14
Morrill, John, 103
Muether, John R., 165
Muller, Richard, 183–84
Myconius, Oswald, 63

Namier, Lewis, 115–16
Newton, Isaac, 144
Nietzsche, 26
Novick, David, 66–67
Novick, Robert, 27–28

Oberman, Heiko, 133, 179
Olson, Lynne, 175–76
Oswald, Lee Harvey, 99
Owen, John, 184

Paul, 80–81
Pfefferkorn, Johannes, 133–34
Plato, 144
Pliny the Younger, 74–81, 119, 148
Polycarp, 132
Popper, Karl, 98, 100

Rassinier, Paul, 30, 33–34
Reuchlin, Johannes, 133–34
Riegner, Gerhard, 59–60
Ritschl, Albrecht, 143
Robertson, Pat, 166
Rushdoony, Rousas, 30
Russell, Conrad, 103
Rutherford, Samuel, 110

Schleiermacher, F. D. E., 143
Schulthess, Johannes, 64–65

Schweizer, Alexander, 64
Scott, Walter, 112
Scotus, John Duns, 128
Servetus, Michael, 189
Service, Robert, 104
Shakespeare, 57
Shaw, George Bernard, 82, 101–2
Shermer, Michael, 33, 35, 37, 44
Shirer, William, 138, 177
Siger of Brabant, 145
Skinner, Quentin, 22, 179–80
Steinmetz, David, 127n2

Tacitus, 178
Thatcher, Margaret, 87, 95n, 155
Thucydide, 178
Todd, Margo, 93n
Torrance, T. F., 145
Trajan, 74–79
Turretin, Francis, 120–29, 139
Tyndale, William, 65, 92

Van Asselt, Willem, 184
Vergil, Polydore, 178
Vico, Giambattista, 178
von Ranke, Leopold, 178–79

Weber, Max, 153–54
William of Occam, 128
Wyclif, John, 188

Zündel, Ernst, 40
Zwingli, Huldrych, 63–65, 94